# THE SOUND
## Guide

## Chaz Celaya

POSITIVE INIFINITY PUBLISHING

*The Sound Guide*
Copyright © 2013 Chaz Celaya

ISBN-13: 978-0615909110

Design by Josie Tennison
Photos by Eleazar Ruiz and Jordan Hawkins
Back Cover Photo by Jeremey Wilson

Celaya, Chaz, 1980 -
The Sound Guide / Chaz Celaya

*Proceeds of this book go to*

MURRIETA MISSION FELLOWSHIP

*Dedicated to those who are expected to do the impossible task of making everyone happy week after week. May your hearts of humble service ultimately make our Father happy and may we all hear Him say "well done good and faithful servant"…*

# Contents

# *Contents*

## Welcome
### Introduction

Hello and welcome to the Sound Guide. First of all, I'm proud of you for actually stopping to read the introduction of a book! The purpose of this book is to equip the people behind the scenes, the ones who somehow get everything to work in the nick of time without anyone knowing any different. Perhaps you have been thrown into this area of service and have no idea where to begin, or maybe you have a decent working knowledge of these things, but have never actually been trained in them, well, you are reading the right book!

If you have served in the audio ministry for any length of time, you probably know by now that you are part of a notoriously thankless area of service. Rarely will people come up after a service and thank you for all the time and effort that goes into facilitating a distraction-free environment for worship. Actually, most people in the church won't even know that you are there until something starts feeding back or a microphone doesn't work, then the church all looks back to see you sweating and red-faced!

Even with its thankless nature, the ministry of audio is of paramount importance in the church today. As the Apostle Paul says in Romans, "Faith comes by hearing, and hearing by the word of God." The church wants to impact the world with the Word of God and what better way than to amplify it, record it, and distribute it, so many can hear it and be changed! Technology should not impede the message, but transparently augment it.

## *Welcome*

### Introduction

As you will hear me say many times in this book, "the key is to be distraction free"; the technology should not get in the way, it should not be accidentally grabbing attention, it should be doing its job in pointing people to Jesus. This doesn't happen on its own, the Lord desires to use you, his set-apart people, to be effective ministers of his Gospel.

My hope is that you can use the fundamentals shown in this guide to establish a solid foundation for service. If any cracks exist in your foundation of audio knowledge, I hope this book can fill them. In fact, as you read through this book you will come across sections labeled "UNLOCK." These are areas where I pinpoint specific terminology and clarify what the terms mean. I trust they will assist you in your journey through the text. May the Lord Jesus bless and equip you both spiritually and practically as you yield your life for his glory.

Chaz Celaya
Murrieta Hot Springs, CA
Summer 2013

# *Section 1.*

## TOOLS OF THE STAGE

I think it's best to start where all the action begins, the stage. The stage is the birthplace of all of the sounds that we will be dealing with. Yes, the stage is like a noise nursery, where at any given moment, tsunamis of sound are developing and being unleashed on our beloved audio equipment. Because of this, it is very important that those working in the sound booth first know all the parts and pieces of the stage.

## KEY TERMS

XLR

¼" Connector

Speak-On Connector

Instrument Cable

Direct Box

Floor Monitor

# TOOLS OF THE STAGE

## BEGINNING

I want to start things out with a brief introduction to some basic terminology. Every specialized field has its own collection of jargon and audio is no exception. Many people get intimidated by fancy words they do not know the meaning of, so in the course of this book I will be seeking to emphasize some of these phrases and explain them in a clear way so that even a musician could understand! This chapter will touch on a few of these terms and we will dive in deeper in later sections.

## COMMUNICATION

Communication is extremely important to any relationship, and so it is with stage musicians and booth techs. From the booth to the stage, we must be on the same page (yes, that rhymes). So let's begin with the objects on stage, the sources of all the noise and the tools we use to capture those beautiful noises.

## CAPTURE TOOLS

### MICROPHONE

We'll talk more in detail about these devices later, but for now, know that micro-phones capture sound waves and convert them to an electrical signal and they use a BALANCED CABLE with an XLR CONNECTOR. We generally just refer to these as MICROPHONE CABLES or simply "XLR's". We also usually simplify "micro-phone" to Mic (pronounced "mike" - no relation to anyone named Mike.)

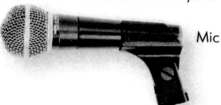

Mic

### GUITAR PICKUP

A device that converts the movement of strings into an electrical signal. Found on electric guitars, electric bass guitars, and most acoustic guitars. Pickups generally employ a ¼" ("QUARTER-INCH") jack that would connect to an UNBALANCED INSTRUMENT CABLE.

Instrument Cable

Electric guitar pickups

## CAPTURE TOOLS (Cont.) ───────────────────────────○

### DIRECT BOX

A device that converts an unbalanced high impedance signal into a balanced low impedance signal. OK, I've already lost you. Simply remember this: When connecting an INSTRUMENT CABLE to the sound system you must go through a DIRECT BOX. We often refer to these as "DI Boxes" (for "Direct Input") or simply a "DI".

Direct Box

## ON A TYPICAL STAGE YOU WILL FIND THE FOLLOWING:

### ACOUSTIC GUITAR

A stringed instrument that is generally plucked with a pick or fingers (I know you already know this, but I figured it would make you feel really smart!). Most acoustic guitars are equipped with a pickup that would use an INSTRUMENT CABLE with a ¼" ("QUARTER-INCH") CONNECTOR.

1/4" Connector

### HELPFUL TIP ───────────────────────────────────○

If an acoustic guitar is used frequently with a sound system it is best to invest in having a pickup installed in the guitar if it does not already have one. Besides the abundant convenience a pickup provides, placing a microphone on the guitar can lead to serious feedback issues, especially when used with a full band.

# TOOLS OF THE STAGE

### ELECTRIC GUITAR AND BASS GUITAR
Electric guitar and Bass guitar generally use amps on stage. Electric guitar amps usually have a microphone placed in front of the speaker of the amp to be heard through the sound system. Electric Bass amps can be mic'ed or a direct box can be used to get the bass signal to the system, since it is generally preferred to have as few mics as necessary on stage.

### ACOUSTIC PIANO/VIOLIN/CELLO
Any acoustic string instrument that doesn't have a pickup installed would need to have a microphone aimed at it to be heard through the system. We'll discuss proper microphone placement later in the book.

### DIGITAL PIANO/SYNTHESIZERS
These electronic instruments can recreate more than just piano sounds. Synthesizers can create an almost innumerable amount of sounds, from strings and horns, to ethereal pads and heavy lead sounds. They generally have a QUARTER-INCH output that would use an INSTRUMENT cable.

### DRUMS/PERCUSSION
There are many different pieces to a standard drum set, and numerous types of percussion instruments like a cajon, djembe, shakers, tambourine, etc. We generally place a microphone on these instruments.

## DRUM SET MAP

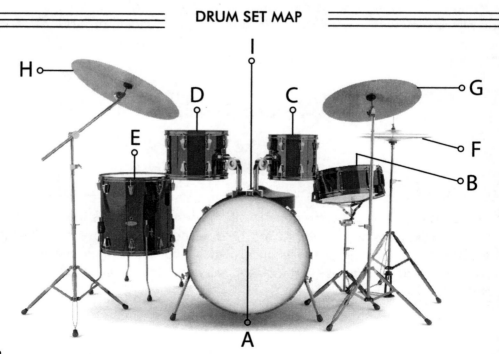

## DRUM SET MAP

A) Bass Drum aka "Kick Drum"

B) Snare Drum

C) High Tom

D) Mid Tom

AKA "Rack Toms"

E) Floor Tom

F) Hi Hat Cymbals

G) Crash Cymbal

H) Ride Cymbal

I) Drum Seat aka "The Throne"

## MONITORS

Up on stage you will generally see some speakers that are designed to sit on the floor and face the ears of the singers and musicians. These are called FLOOR MONITORS aka STAGE WEDGES. (Audio engineers used to call these FOLDBACK speakers) The purpose of these speakers is to provide a means for the performers to hear themselves and other people in the band so that they can play together comfortably and hopefully stay in tune and in time. Floor Monitors are connected using a SPEAKER CABLE with ¼" or preferably, SPEAK-ON CONNECTORS.

Floor monitors can be replaced by In Ear Monitors (IEM's or "In-Ears"), a monitor worn in the ear like a headphone earbud. We will discuss this further in a later section.

Floor Monitor

Speak-on Connector

## *Conclusion*

These are the common pieces you will find on a stage and the terms used to describe them. Of course every church, every stage, and every sound system is different (and can vary greatly from one day to the next), but despite the setup or arrangement, you will be receiving sound into the system from either a microphone or a direct box.

Now that we're familiar with some of the tools used to create and capture sound waves, let's take a moment to discuss the actual sound waves themselves and how they function.

# NOTES

# *Section 2.*

―――――――――――――――
―――――――――――――――

## THE WONDER OF SOUND

Sound...it comes at us 24 hours a day for our entire lives. It is an endless stream of information feeding directly into our heads, but we don't seem to mind it, actually we find it quite useful, and sometimes even enjoyable. Knowing how these sound waves work; how they travel from their point of conception to their eventual destination (apart from any sound equipment) is extremely important and will be the topic of this section.

### KEY TERMS

Sound

Amplitude

Decibel (dB)

Frequency

Hertz (Hz)

# THE WONDER OF SOUND

*Let everyone in the world fear the Lord, And let everyone
stand in awe of him. For when he spoke, the world
began! It appeared at his command.*
*(Psalm 33:8,9)*

---

Sound is an amazing creation. From the psalm above we see that God himself was the initiator of the first sound this world has ever known. He SPOKE and the world began! God has designed sound, from the production of a sound, to the propagation of the sound wave, and to the eventual perception by the hearer. **It's a beautiful process**

Let's begin with what sound actually is: a molecular disturbance that is heard by the human ear. Despite the fact that sound can travel through water and solids, we primarily deal with sound that is traveling through the gaseous mixture we commonly call "air".

## SOUND IS LIKE A DOMINO

Whenever a sound is heard, let's say a sneeze for instance, there was a starting point that set off a massive chain reaction, something disturbed some quietly resting molecules and made them move around, and as they moved they bumped into other molecules, which in turn, disturbed their neighboring molecules. Eventually, like people doing the "wave" at a baseball stadium, this molecular commotion travels across the room and reaches our eardrum. Eardrums, by no mere coincidence, are extremely sensitive to molecular change and, in fact, start to move right along with the "wave". Connected to the other side of our eardrums we have a tiny crank-shaft-like mechanism made up of the three smallest bones in our body, so as our eardrum moves, this crank-shaft moves as well. The last bone in the mechanism is connected to a fluid-filled sack roughly the size of a grape (technically it's called the cochlea). So now our stadium-wave molecular commotion has made it to this fluid-filled sack, which in turn sets the fluid in motion. Inside the cochlea are thousands of tiny hair cells, which are connected to our auditory nerve. So now, like in a microphone, the molecular disturbance has been converted into an electrical impulse that shoots right into the auditory cortex of our brain, where it is processed and we respond with "bless you!".

**WHY IS SOUND IMPORTANT?** Well, the way our ears interpret different sound waves is really what all of sound engineering boils down to. "Does it sound good?" Can be a very relative standard, but knowing the basic principles of how these sounds waves work, and how the equipment we use can manipulate these waves is critical to our audio knowledge.

16

## SOUND WAVE CHARACTERISTICS

A big question we need to answer is: what differentiates one sound wave from another? Let's say we are listening to the mix at church one week and think, "that sounds great" and the next week we hear it and think, "that sounds terrible" – what has changed in the sound waves that are entering our beloved ear canals? Well, there are seven primary characteristics of sound waves that cause a differentiation in our sonic perception. Just like people have different hair color, body shapes, skin tones, etc. so do sound waves, but we don't call it hair color, we have other names for these characteristics, they are:

## 1. AMPLITUDE

Amplitude is the relative strength of a sound wave. We might describe it as how tall a sound wave is. The taller the sound wave (the more amplitude it has) the LOUDER our ears perceive it to be. We can actually measure the amplitude of a sound wave. When we do, we use a unit called a Decibel. We generally abbreviate this to "dB". The dB unit is a very common one, seen all over audio equipment, so remember it.

**Remember: the more dB's = the LOUDER it will be to our ears.**

## UNLOCK ━━━━━━━━━━━━━━━━━━━━━━━━━━━━━━━━━━━━━━ ⚷

Since the decibel is a common unit of measurement in science and electronics, there are different suffixes attached to "dB" to specify what exactly is being measured. Audio equipment uses "dBu" – a measurement of voltage. When we are talking about acoustic sound waves we are specifically referring to dB SPL (which stands for "Sound Pressure Level." Often when discussing the strength or intensity of acoustic sounds, people may simply refer to them as "SPL's"). ━━━━━━━━━━━━━━━━━━━━━━━━━━━━━━━━━━━━━━━

To get a feel of how much a decibel is, look at the decibel level chart. You'll see I placed an amount of time next to a few of the levels. This marks how much time your ears can take getting bombarded with sound waves that size before we start suffering hearing loss. **Never forget that the most important tool in a sound persons arsenal is not the microphones, the mixer, or the main speakers – it's your EARS!** If your ears don't work, then your days dialing in the mix are probably over and it's time to see what the Lord has for you in the next season of ministry. If God has entrusted you with a functional set of ears then be a good steward of them, and don't expose them to unneeded damage. It's also good for a sound person to remember that it's not being a blessing to the people in your congregation if you inflict them with hearing loss on a weekly basis. So it's beneficial to have a dB meter (or a dB meter app on your smartphone), so you can check the level of your mix during worship.

# THE WONDER OF SOUND

194: Shock Waves
165: Shotgun
135: Jet Plane (from 100 feet)
130: Threshold of Pain
125: Ambulance, Jack Hammer
115: Leaf Blower, Rock Concert (30 seconds)
110: Power Saw 1 Minute, 29 seconds
100: iPod at high volume (15 minutes)
 94: Lawn Mower, Hair Dryer (1hour)
 85: City Traffic (8 hours)
 75: Washing Machine
 60: Typical Speech
 50: Rainfall
 20: Whisper
  0: Softest Sound the Ear can Hear

**Remember:** the dB meter is simply a reference tool, it won't tell you if your mix is "good" or not, it will just tell you the strength of the sound waves coming from your speakers. The goal shouldn't be a loud mix or quiet mix, the goal should be a good mix. Yes, a loud hearing-loss-inducing mix is a bad thing for the congregation, but a mix that is too quiet is also a bad thing. **That's because a quiet mix can be awkward.** Most people are already a bit self-conscious about singing in public. If the mix is too quiet they will feel overly conspicuous and their singing will become inhibited as a result. This is a prime example of technology that can actually prove to be a disservice and a distraction. There are times when the music is supposed to be in the background (like during a time of prayer, or exit music) so, of course, your mix should be quiet in those instances, but if it's not supposed to be background music, then your mix shouldn't sound like it.

## UNLOCK

It's important to note that the decibel is a logarithmic unit, not a linear one. What does that even mean you ask? Well, it means that as you go up the decibel chart things will get very loud very quickly. For every 3dB increase in SPL, the increase in sound pressure is actually doubled. This is why you can be exposed to 94dB for one hour, but 97dB for only 30 minutes, and 100dB is only 15 minutes. A 3dB increase means double the strength, resulting in half of the exposure time before possible hearing loss.

## 2. FREQUENCY

Frequency is what our ears perceive as the "pitch" of a sound. Does it sound high pitched like a flute or is it low pitched like a tuba? We measure frequency in a unit called Hertz, and we abbreviate it "Hz". (You will see an "Hz" knob in the EQ section of your sound board, go ahead and look) When we are measuring Hertz we are actually measuring how many full cycles a sound wave completes in 1 second of time. (sometimes frequency is referred to as "Cycles Per Second" for this reason). The more cycles per second (or Hz), the higher the perceived pitch.

**Less cycles per second = less Hz = lower/deeper the perceived sound.**

**Human ears cannot hear every possible frequency.** The range of human hearing is 20Hz to 20,000Hz. Anything below 20Hz we call "subsonic" because it's too low to be heard with our ears, and anything above 20,000Hz we call ultrasonic. In the tight confines of a mixing console it would take too much surface space to print "20,000Hz" so we abbreviate a thousand cycles as "k" (for kilohertz). So we would say the range of human hearing is: 20Hz to 20kHz.

When it comes to operating a mixing console, these first two characteristics are the most important. Practically EVERY knob and fader on the entire mixing console is to adjust either dB or Hz!!

## 3. WAVELENGTH

Wavelength is the physical size of a sound wave (yes, sound waves are real, physical things, you just don't see them). The lower the frequency (Hz, remember?) The longer the wavelength.

A 20Hz wave has a wavelength of 56 feet (that's for a single cycle!)
A 20kHz wave has a wavelength of .6 inches

Because of the actual size, high frequencies are easily absorbed as they travel. Things like walls, chairs, people, etc. Can easily absorb high frequencies, whereas lower frequency waves are very difficult to absorb or control.

## 4. VELOCITY

Velocity is the speed of the sound wave. Sound waves travel through air at an average speed of 343 meters per second (or 1125 feet per second), that calculates to roughly 767 miles per hour. With sound waves coming at your face at that speed all day long, it's no wonder you're tired by the end of the day. The speed of sound does vary by two primary things: the material it is traveling through (Increased density = Increased speed, so it travels faster through water) and the air temperature (Increased Temperature = Increased speed).

### It's Important To Note

The speed of sound, while fast in car standards, is still slow enough to cause trouble. For instance, say you have an extra set of speakers set up in the balcony of your sanctuary, the sound waves from those speakers will reach the listener's ears before the sound waves from the main speakers/stage. The difference could only be milliseconds, but this will lead to a distinct lack of clarity and intelligibility for the people listening in the balcony.

# THE WONDER OF SOUND

## 5. ENVELOPE

Envelope is the lifespan of the sound wave. Some sounds are short, they abruptly happen then are gone (like hitting a snare drum), while others are long and can sustain for a long period of time (like bowing a violin). Every sound wave has an attack (when the sound wave starts) and a decay (the time it takes to completely die out). The initial attack of a sound (sometimes referred to as the "TRANSIENT") is very important to how our ears perceive the sound. Actually if you were to remove the transients from the sound waves of different instruments it would be very hard to tell one instrument apart from another.

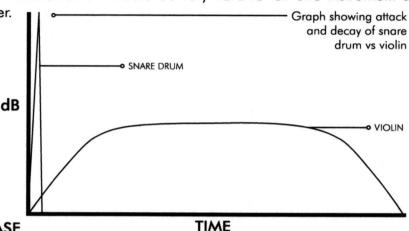

Graph showing attack and decay of snare drum vs violin

dB

SNARE DRUM

VIOLIN

TIME

## 6. PHASE

Phase deals with the timing and shape of a sound wave. In sound we can encounter phase issues whenever we have two microphones on a single sound source (like drum overheads or choir mics). If the timing between the two waves becomes off, they start to cancel out frequencies between them (usually making it sound thin and sometimes very weird). If two sound waves of the same frequency are perfectly 180° out of phase you have phase cancellation and you won't hear either of the sound waves!

## 7. TIMBRE

Timbre (I have seen much debate in regards to the pronunciation of this word, but it is generally pronounced with an "o" sound like "Tom – bur" or alternatively, with a long "a" like the first two syllables of the word "tambourine") refers to the overall tonal qualities of a sound. Many factors contribute to the timbre of a sound, from transients to the overtones produced by the instrument or sound source. Why does a saxophone sound like a sax and nothing like a piano? What if they played the exact same note (Hz) at the exact same loudness (dB)? We could all still tell the difference between a sax and a piano right? (I hope you said yes). Our ears can tell the difference between a sound wave created from a vibrating wooden reed that is resonating a brass tube (aka the sax), and a vibrating steel string that has been hit with a felt hammer (the piano).

20

# *Conclusion* ─────────────────────────────────o

Congratulations, you survived the synopsis of how sound waves work! Hopefully this little bit of science hasn't discouraged you from the audio ministry altogether! Now that we know how sound waves work in their natural environment, we'll look at how we capture them and get them into the ears of the congregation.

# NOTES

# Section 3.

## THE PATH OF SOUND

I'd venture to say that 50% of a sound person's job comes down to troubleshooting - making something work when it's not. By far, the biggest aid to a soundperson's troubleshooting ability is to simply know the signal path, the route the sound travels from point A (the microphone on stage) to point B (the speakers), and in our case, even to point C (the listener's ears).

## KEY TERMS

Stage Box

Snake

Main EQ/System Processor

House Mix

Mic Level

Line Level

Front of House

# THE PATH OF SOUND

All sound systems serve the same basic purpose and that is to AMPLIFY! Yes, they all simply capture the sound waves created on stage and amplify them (make them louder) so people anywhere in the room can hear everything clearly.

Most sound systems will vary in size and specific equipment, and the rooms they are installed in are all different, but from one sound system to the next you will still have the same basic components.

## BASIC SIGNAL PATH FOR A SOUND SYSTEM

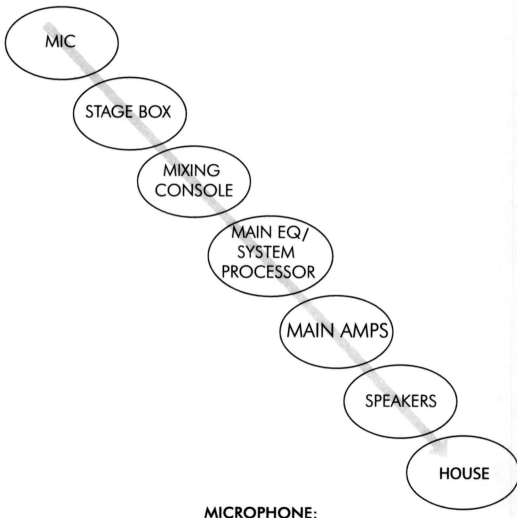

- MIC
- STAGE BOX
- MIXING CONSOLE
- MAIN EQ/ SYSTEM PROCESSOR
- MAIN AMPS
- SPEAKERS
- HOUSE

### MICROPHONE:

Captures the acoustic sound waves moving through the air and converts them into an electric voltage. (Or DI BOX: Converts unbalanced cable to balanced cable)

Connect via XLR to the...

## STAGE BOX

(As the name suggests) it is a box on stage with numerous sequentially numbered female XLR jack inputs, these are the sound sources you are sending to the mixing console so we call them SENDS.  FYI: The stage box usually has some outputs as well; they call these RETURNS since they are used to return audio to the stage from the mixing console (useful for monitor mixes!).

Connects to the...

## SNAKE

available in both analog and digital versions, the snake carries all of your xlr inputs over a single cable.  It's a clean and orderly solution for running multiple cables over a long distance.

Connects to the

## MIXING CONSOLE

The hub where all of the sound sources from stage meet and are blended together into sweet sounding mixes that are sent to the stage, audience, and anywhere else you want them to go.

Connects via XLR's to the...

## MAIN EQ/SYSTEM PROCESSOR

depending on the specific unit (they vary widely or can even be built into the console itself), this allows you to make EQ adjustments to your overall mix, thus tailoring the sound to better suit your specific room. Sometimes a device can do much more than simply provide EQ adjustments, it can give you tools like compression, limiting, speaker delay, etc (stuff we'll be talking about later!)

Connects via XLR's to the...

# THE PATH OF SOUND

## MAIN AMPLIFIERS

The main amplifiers have one specific job in life: to amplify! They take your beautiful mix and boost its signal enough to power the speakers.

Connect to the...

## SPEAKERS

They, like the opposite of a microphone, take our amplified electrical voltage and convert it back into an acoustic sound wave.

Connects via sound waves to the...

## THE HOUSE

Besides the multiple stage mixes we have going on for the musicians, we also have our most important mix, the one for the audience. This is referred to as the HOUSE MIX.

**UNLOCK**

**There are a few "2in1" exceptions to this path,** such as a POWERED SPEAKER (aka ACTIVE SPEAKER) these are speakers with the amplifiers built into them (so two devices in one!). There are also POWERED MIXERS: which are mixing console with the amplifiers built into them.

As stated earlier, most digital mixing consoles will also have main EQ and some system processing features built into them as well. But, even with devices being more consolidated in our modern age, the signal still must travel through those stages to eventually reach its destination.

**TROUBLESHOOTING TIP:** The output of one device plugs into the input of the next device in the path. It's like links in a chain, so when something is not working and you have to troubleshoot a problem, use your knowledge of the signal path to narrow down what link in the chain has been broken. This is why you MUST KNOW the entire signal path of your system. Even if it was installed 15 years ago and no one has ever explained it to you, take 10 minutes and follow the whole path of your system from beginning to end.

## Know Your Level Types!! Not All Inputs and Outputs are Equal

As your signal travels from the microphone to the speakers it gets stepped up in power, so it is NOT THE SAME as it travels down the signal path. So just because you can plug a cable into another device does not mean they are intended to work together.

Here's a quick and simple breakdown of level types:

### MIC LEVEL

The output of a microphone, it is the weakest signal we work with(roughly -30dBu)

### INSTRUMENT LEVEL

The output from instrument pickups (roughly -20 dBu) DI Box inputs are designed for this

### LINE LEVEL

The output of mic pre-amps and mixing consoles (consumer gear is -10dBu, professional gear is +4dBu). Headphone Level: a form of line level that is optimized to power headphones.

### SPEAKER LEVEL

Signal that is amplified enough to drive large loud speakers. Always ensure the output level of a device matches the intended input level of the next device in the chain.

**For Example**

I commonly see people have issues with this when using portable powered speakers. Powered speakers are generally equipped with at least one XLR input that can be set to either a "Mic-In" or a "Line-In". If you are plugging a microphone directly

into the XLR input of the speaker then switch the input to "Mic-In", but if you are plugging the output of a mixing console into the XLR input of the powered speaker then be sure the input is switched to "Line-In". Plugging a line-level signal into a mic-level input can create nasty feedback!

The Mic/Line input selector switch on a powered speaker

# THE PATH OF SOUND

## THE STAGE MONITOR SIGNAL PATH

In many churches the person doing the house mix is also the one responsible for adjusting the stage mixes as well, so it would be wise to also know the signal path for the monitors. If you are running stage mixes from the front of house* mix console then your stage mix signal path will include the AUX Bus aka "AUX SENDS". AUX SENDS (short for "Auxiliary Sends") are simply additional outputs from the mixer that can be used to send individual inputs from the stage to other devices (like stage monitors, IEM's, FX processors, recorders, foyer feeds, web streams ,etc) .

## UNLOCK

A sound person generally deals with 3 worlds: The stage, the house (where the audience is), and the sound booth. The sound booth is usually referred to as the FRONT OF HOUSE often abbreviated to FOH.

## BREAKING DOWN THE MONITOR SIGNAL PATH

Let's say we have a drummer who needs more acoustic guitar in their monitor mix. The guitar is plugged into channel 7 on the board and the drummer's stage mix is plugged into Aux Send 4. Signal comes from the guitar, into a DI, to the stage box, through the snake, to the mixer. Since the drummer has requested more guitar in their mix I need to go to the channel on the board that has the guitar coming in (Channel 7). On the channel strip of Channel 7 there will be a knob for Aux 4. The more I turn the knob for Aux 4 on Channel 7 the more acoustic guitar signal is sent to Aux 4, which then goes to the Aux 4 Master knob. On the back on the console will be an Aux Send 4 output jack (usually a ¼" or XLR connector) where the signal can go to a Master Monitor EQ, then to an amp **(these are separate EQ's and amps from our main mix signal path)** that would then power a stage monitor speaker.

## HOW TO SEND AUDIO TO A SPECIFIC MONITOR
**What sound does the player want?**
(Go to that channel)

**What aux send is the player's mix on?**
(Go to that aux send on the channel of the sound they want)

Some digital consoles are laid out in such a way that these steps would be opposite, so make sure you have studied up on your individual console!

28

## There Are Generally Two Expections To Monitors Being Mixed From FOH

1) Your church is equipped with a split-snake, where you have a second console next to the stage specifically for running stage mixes (common in concert venues and festivals, but rare in the local church due to the added expense and space of a second console along with the necessity for a second trained operator of said second console) and,

2) Your church is equipped with a personal monitor mixing system, where the musicians on stage are equipped with personal mixers to adjust their own individual mixes. This is becoming increasingly common, especially with the ability of some digital consoles to be controlled wirelessly with a smartphone or tablet device.

## MONITOR MIXES: THE SOURCE OF THE PROBLEM

If there is ever a reason for discord between the stage people and the sound people, monitor mixes would probably sit atop the list. Remember: The purpose of monitors is to assist the players on stage, giving them the ability to hear the other members of the band so they can play and sing IN TUNE and IN TIME.

The problem with a stage monitor being too loud is that it muddies our house mix! Yes muddies, (as in adds mud), it makes our house mix less clear and defined. You see, when sound waves leave the monitors on stage they are traveling AWAY from the house towards the back wall of the stage, where they hit the wall, have all of their high frequencies absorbed by the wall, and then bounce out to add to the house mix nothing but low-mid and low frequencies. We then have to try and compensate for this by turning the vocals up in the house so that they don't get lost in the mud bath. What results is a really bad sounding mix where everything is too loud! Sound familiar?

Because of this, we want to do everything we can to keep the stage volume from ruining the house mix, while also giving the musicians everything they need to do what they are called to do. Once again, it doesn't mean our goal is a silent stage, it means we need to be proactive about keeping stage volume from getting out of hand and becoming a distraction.

## WAYS TO KEEP STAGE VOLUME DOWN

1) First, it's best to give the players on stage only what they need in their mixes, if they don't ask for something, then don't assume they want it. Also, there are times when someone might want more of something (usually themselves) in their mix, but I have no more to give from the board, so I'll turn down something else in their mix with the hopes that it will allow them to hear more of what they want. Remember to always ask and ensure that the musician is comfortable with their mix.

# THE PATH OF SOUND

**2) In-Ear Monitors:** These allow for floor monitors and instead put the mix directly in the musician's ears. And remember, the fewer floor monitors on stage the better

**You have 3 types of IEM's: Headphones, Universal fit, Custom molds**

### HEADPHONES

OK, these of course are not "in-ear" monitors but rather "over the ear". A good pair of closed-back headphones will sound great, are relatively affordable and usually pretty comfortable as well. These work great for drummers since drummers don't move around very much.

### UNIVERSAL FIT

These are a cylindrical-shaped ear bud type headphone that fits into your ear with a better fit and seal than a standard round ear-bud. These often have removable or replaceable tips so that you can keep them fresh after your ear wax has defiled them.

### CUSTOM FIT

These are earphones that have been custom-shaped to fit your ear canal exactly. You have to go to an audiologist to get the molds done, then you send the molds to your vendor of choice. These are, of course, the best fitting ear buds you'll ever have, and they sound great. These used to be astronomically expensive, but the price points have come down dramatically on them and they are now attainable to the common man.

## TRANSITIONING TO IN-EAR MONITORS

As a musician who uses IEM's I can testify that it takes some getting used to. Initially it feels very isolated and like you're not in the same room as everyone else. **The key to using IEM's is having a good mix!**

## MIXING IN-EARS

The sound person must realize that providing a mix to someone with In-Ears is a different ballgame than with a floor wedge. First of all, YOU CAN DO A LOT OF DAMAGE to a person's hearing if you are not careful. Accidental feedback can be punishing if wearing In-Ears and the sound person must be extra careful to prevent it. It is wise to make sure a limiter (discussed in a later section) is on every channel feeding an IEM. Most In-Ear wireless systems have limiters built-in as well. You will need a lot more in your mix with In-Ears because the ear pieces themselves work like ear-plugs and block out all the natural sounds on stage you are used to, so plan on it taking a bit more time to dial in the IEM mix. Also, an ambient microphone is critical for providing the sense of being back in the same room as everyone

else. AMBIENT MICROPHONES are mics set up on stage specifically for an in-ear mix. You always want to make absolutely sure that these mics are never fed through to your house mix! It's best to use a condenser microphone for this and place it close to where the musicians are on stage. A musician can add as much or as little of the ambiance as they like, but it definitely helps them to feel like they back in the room. Lastly, if possible, a stereo In-Ear mix is a big help in getting used to the transition. A stereo mix gives you the ability to pan individual sounds to one ear or the other. It widens the sound of your mix and makes it feel much more natural. The ability of IEM's to be stereo gives them a huge advantage over a standard mono floor wedge.

## HELPFUL SOLUTIONS FOR IN-EAR MONITORS

A) "HeadTap" - simple & inexpensive box that allows you to convert a speaker level signal to a headphone – level. Just unplug the speak-on from the monitor, plug it in to this box, plug headphones into the box, and presto, you have a headphone mix instead of a floor monitor!

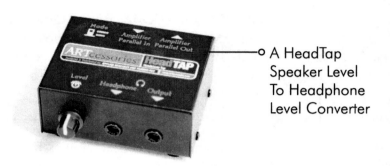

A HeadTap
Speaker Level
To Headphone
Level Converter

## HELPFUL SOLUTIONS FOR IN-EAR MONITORS (Cont.)

**B) Personal Monitor Mixing System -** Allows the musicians to set their own monitor levels, thus freeing the soundperson to focus on the house mix! These are best utilized with In-Ear Monitors.

**C) Digital Mixers -** Some digital sound boards will allow multiple wireless devices (phones/tablets) to connect and control levels remotely, thus enabling the device-equipped musicians to control their own mix, and the tablet-equipped soundperson can mix from anywhere in the room!

**D) Wireless System -** If a musician doesn't like the feeling of being tied down to a cable you can plug your Aux Send output into a wireless transmitter. The musician wears the beltpack receiver with IEM's plugged into it. I've found that you usually get what you pay for with wireless systems, so cheap ones will usually sound that way and more expensive systems will sound more natural.

**3) Deal with drums! -** When it comes to volume, drums are always public enemy number one, and logically so since they are, acoustically speaking, the loudest instrument on stage.

A) Avoid setting up drums in the corner of a room – it creates an amphitheater-type affect on the sound waves, which makes the drums louder.

B) Use smaller sticks, drums and cymbals: "Hot-Rods" (dowel-type sticks) and thinner sticks help reduce volume along with smaller sized drums and cymbals.

C) Always have a rug or carpet under the drum kit.

D) Make sure your drummer knows that Dynamics and Tempo are independent qualities in music. I've had drummers who think that asking them to play quiet means it's impossible to play an upbeat song, this is an absurdity. It is possible to play quiet without having to play slow.

E) Drum Shields & Fish Tanks: The drum shield is a plexi-glass divider that helps to prevent the drum sounds from bleeding into other microphones (especially vocal mics) on stage. People tend to think these will magically make the drums quieter, and they soon find out they were sadly mistaken. Drum shields provide some additional ISOLATION (keeping the sounds out of other mics), which is good if you find that every time you turn up the lead vocal you are actually turning up the snare drum along with it, but drum shields do not provide ABSORPTION. Absorption actually reduces the energy of sound waves. This is where the fish tanks come in. There are drum isolation booths available that actually surround the drums set with a combination of absorptive panels and clear panels (so you can still see the drummer in all of his sweaty glory - it can get hot in those isolation booths). I have truly seen this work well in certain situations, but never assume that locking the drummer away in a padded cell will instantly solve the problem. Once you have the drummer locked away, it is now UP TO YOU, the sound person, to make the drums sound alive and natural in your room. Remember, the goal isn't "Quiet Drums!" the goal is a good non-distracting mix. So know the tools at your disposal and use them to their best advantage.

**4) Electric guitars:** use low-wattage tube amps (15 watts or less) to get the warm "tube tone" at lower volume levels. Put the amp on a tilt back stand facing the guitarist's head (you know, that big thing where his ears are), so he doesn't have to turn it up as loud to hear himself. It's usually not a good idea to have the amp sitting on the stage, pointed directly at the audience because the sound waves from the amp will go right past the guitarist's knees and directly into the faces of the people in the front row. So the poor folks in the front row will only get to hear drums and electric guitar! You can even mic the amp offstage in a separate room, or surround it with some sound-absorption panels, and send it through people's stage mixes for even better control.

Guitar amp on a tiltback stand, with rear absoption panel

**5) Bass Amps:**The bass doesn't need to power the house from his amp on stage. His amp on stage just needs to be loud enough for the bass player to hear himself. The bass is DI'd into the sound system so the sound person can control the level in the house.

## *Conclusion*

There are options like amp simulators for electric guitars and basses that enable you to do away with amps on stage entirely. These are totally fine if you can dial in a good tone and everyone is comfortable with it, but remember (one more time) the goal isn't necessarily a sterile and silent stage, the goal is a good distraction-free mix.

# NOTES

# Section 4.

## MIXING CONSOLE

People tend to really panic when it comes to the console, and rightly so. It is the centerpiece of the sound system, it's flashy with bright lights and a seemingly countless array of knobs, buttons, and faders. To be the person standing behind such a marvel of modern engineering is a sign of ultimate authority and intelligence (at least we like to think so). You can do a lot with a mixing board these days, but if you don't know how to operate it, you will only want to crawl underneath the shiny console and hide when things start going wrong. So let's break down the console, de-mystify it, and aim to use it to its full potential.

### KEY TERMS

Channel Strip

Master Section

Gain

Lo-Cut/High Pass Filter

Pre-Fader Send

Post-Fader Send

SubGroups

Mute-Groups

## BEGINNING

The biggest challenge with training someone on mixing consoles is that every console is different, and it seems like new models are coming out every other week. I can't teach you in one simple section how to use every mixing console ever designed, but I can familiarize you with the standard signal flow of a console and the standard buttons and knobs found on most consoles, why they are there and what they do. So whether your console is old or new, analog or digital, small or large, you will likely encounter the following terminology. So here we go:

### There are two Sections of a Mixing console:
### The Channel Strip & The Master Section

1) The Channel Strip: Each input from the stage box gets its own channel strip and the channel strip is where you can make adjustments to that individual signal.

**Rule #1 when working with mixing consoles**: if you know one channel, you know them all. Consoles come in all shapes and sizes, you generally see them ranging from 4 channels to 40 channels. There are some exceptions, but once you know what all the knobs and buttons do on one individual channel, then you pretty much know the rest of them on the entire board.

2) The Master Section: It's the section of the console where all of the "Master" knobs are, very useful for making large volume adjustments with minimal effort. Most of the features found in the master section are designed to give you more options and flexibility along with making your overall mixing task a lot easier and efficient, so it's good to know what the stuff in the Master Section is all about!

Master Section
On an Analog
Console

**Let's start by looking at the Channel Strip first**
It is divided into 4 main sections:
Input
EQ
Aux Sends
Output

**Digital Consoles** will usually give you an additional section for dynamics featuring added processing like a noise gate, compressor, limiter, etc. These consoles will generally have the aux sends in a different section as well, not necessarily in the channel strip like an analog board, thus you will still have 4 sections to the channel strip!

# MIXING CONSOLE

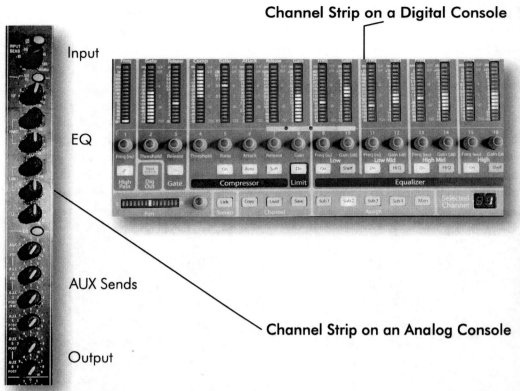

**Channel Strip on a Digital Console**

Input

EQ

AUX Sends

**Channel Strip on an Analog Console**

Output

## Input Section:
In the Input section you will generally see the following jacks/knobs/switches

## UNLOCK
"Knob" is a pretty generic word for the round control generally used to make adjustments to settings on a mixing console or other device. The knob is actually controlling what's called a "potentiometer" so the slang term used most often for knob is "pot". (Like what you plant flowers in).

## GAIN SENSITIVITY
(Console manufacturers will sometimes also refer to this knob as "Input Sensitivity" or "Trim") I say without hesitation that this is THE MOST IMPORTANT piece of your channel strip. I'll say it again to let you know that I really mean it: properly setting the Gain pot will make or break your mix!!! If you don't know how to set gain properly, it will be discussed in the next section, so you might want to read ahead! As your sound source has come down the signal path from the stage and entered the console it is very weak and is in need of a boost, so there's a little amplifier at the beginning of the channel strip that allows us to boost the signal to a usable level. The gain pot is simply controlling this little amplifier, allowing us to dial-in the best setting for the particular sound source on that channel.

**UNLOCK** ———————————————————————•

The little amplifier that boosts the microphone signal at the start of a channel is called a MICROPHONE PRE-AMP, oftentimes referred to as a MIC-PRE for short. The name derives from the fact that it is an amplifier, but not the main amplifier that is powering the speakers, since it comes before the main amplifier it is the "pre"-amplifier. This little device plays an extremely important role in your signal path, since it must boost the signal without adding any additional noise or degrading the sound in any way. Oftentimes what makes the difference between a decent console and a great console are its mic-pre's.———————————————

### INSERT

A ¼" jack that acts as both a send AND a return when used with an insert cable.

### DIRECT OUT

A ¼" jack that allows you to split the signal from the channel and send it to another device. Useful for connecting to personal monitor mixing systems or recording devices

### LINE IN

¼" connector for line-level sources (like an mp3 player, computer, DVD player, etc)

### PAD (Not Pictured)

The pad switch attenuates (aka reduces, or turns down) the level of the signal coming in. Helpful when you have a line level signal coming into the microphone input.

### +48V

Phantom Power switch, MUST be on for condenser microphones or active direct boxes to work.

### MIC IN

A female XLR connector for mic cables (this is where the snake would plug in).

## UNLOCK

An INSERT CABLE is a "Y" shaped cable with a ¼" TRS (stereo) connector that splits into two TS (mono) connectors. One of the connectors (the tip) acts as a send, while the other connector (the ring) works as a return. When used with an insert jack on a console, the insert cable can send signal from the channel to an outboard processor (like a compressor) and back again.

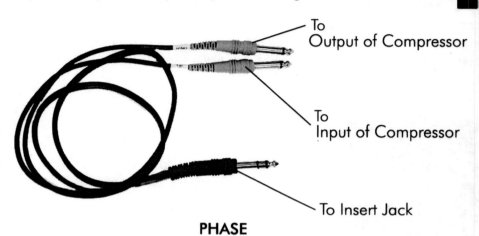

To
Output of Compressor

To
Input of Compressor

To Insert Jack

## PHASE

This button will invert the phase of the incoming signal by 180°. If you are having phasing issues with a stereo sound source (which would be two signals coming in on 2 separate channels) then try pushing this button on one of the channels and listen for a difference.

## LO-CUT AKA HIGH PASS FILTER OR HPF

for the sake of space on the console, this button is usually marked by just a simple symbol. When you activate the HPF you are basically turning down everything from 100Hz down on that channel. Different consoles will have a different preset frequency, or allow you to choose the cutoff frequency, but it is generally @ 100Hz. Very few instruments or voices produce any usable sonic information below 100Hz so it's good to use the HPF on most channels of your console. The kick drum and the bass guitar are the primary sources for the extreme low end in your mix so DON'T use the HPF on these channels, that would also apply to any channels where backing tracks, loops, or pre-recorded music are coming through. Sometimes you'll want some bigger low end from a piano/synth or floor tom as well, so use it to taste. Be sure to use the HPF on all of your vocal mics and drum overheads. You will notice an immediate clearing up of your mix, along with fewer feedback issues!

**low cut symbol** (aka HPF)

**UNLOCK** ——————————————————————————————————————🔑
Since The High Pass Filter is cutting out the low frequencies it is sometimes called a lo-cut, but another way to look at it is that it is putting a filter in the signal that catches lows while allowing the high frequencies to pass through (hence the name "high pass filter" and abbreviated HPF). ————————————————————————🔓

○——————— **In the EQ Section you will see knobs for the** ———————○

Phase

Gain

HPF

### HIGH
Pot that will boost or cut the high frequencies in the signal

### FREQUENCY KNOB
Selects the frequency you wish to boost or cut.

### HIGH MID'S
Pot that will boost or cut the upper mid-range frequencies selected with the frequency selector knob.

### LOW MID'S
Pot that will boost or cut the lower mid-range frequencies selected with the frequency selector knob.

### LOW
Pot that will boost or cut the low frequencies in the signal
EQ In/Out: switch that activates the EQ controls. If this is switched off then you can move the knobs all you want, bu you won't hear any change whatsoever. If you console doesn't have a switch then your EQ is always in.

### EQ IN/OUT
switch that activates the EQ controls. If this is switched off then you can move the knobs all you want, but you won't hear any change whatsoever. If your console doesn't have a switch then your EQ is always in.

# MIXING CONSOLE

In the **Aux Send** section you will see a pot for each aux send. The number of aux sends will vary depending on the number your mixer is equipped with. It can be anywhere from 2 to 20+

## UNLOCK ————————————————————————————●━

There are two TYPES OF AUX SENDS: PRE-FADER and POST-FADER.

The levels of the PRE-FADER aux send are independent of changes made to the channel output fader. So anytime levels are being adjusted for the house mix, the levels of the pre-fader aux sends DO NOT CHANGE. Whereas levels on a POST-FADER aux send are affected by changes made to the house mix. Therefore, it is imperative that all stage mixes must be on pre-fader aux sends. Having a stage mix on a post-fader aux send will lead to all-out chaos on stage, so Just Don't Do It. So why have Post-Fader aux sends? Post-fade sends are for when you want the levels to change along with the levels in the house mix. They are great to use for FX sends and for sends to sub-woofers. ————————————————————

## Output Section ————————————————————————————○

### PAN

Directs the output signal to either the Left or Right output. When using subgroups the pan pot can specify which subgroup a channel is assigned to.

### ASSIGNMENT BUTTONS

Assigns where the channel will output to, either to a subgroup or directly to the main output faders.

### MUTE

Completely silences the output of the channel (you know, like the mute button on your TV)

### MUTE ASSIGNMENTS

Assigns the channel to a mute group, if your console is equipped with mute groups (not all consoles have these)

### SOLO/PRE-FADER LISTEN AKA PFL

Allows you to listen to a selected channel through the headphones without disturbing your main mix.

### FADER

Adjusts the output level from the channel to your house mix

## LABEL STRIP

Area where a strip of sound board tape is placed so you can label what is on that channel. It's too easy to forget what is plugged in where, and in the fast-paced environment of Live Sound it is always a wise idea to label your console channels. On a digital board with layers of channels, the console should have a customizable screen so you can still label each channel (without having to use tape).

## IN THE MASTER SECTION YOU WILL FIND

## SUBGROUPS

Subgroups simplify the mixing process by enabling you to assign multiple channel faders to a single fader. For example: you can assign all the channels for your drums mics to subgroup 1, thus allowing you to control the volume of the entire drumset using the single subgroup 1 fader instead of the 8 or so faders for the drum mics.

### UNLOCK

Some consoles do not have subgroups, but instead will have VCA's (Voltage-Controlled Amplifier) or DCA's (Digital-Controlled Amplifier). Each of these is different in their functionality, but the basic concept is the same in that you are able to control multiple channels with a single fader, so don't be afraid to use them!

## MUTE GROUPS

Mute groups simplify the mixing process by enabling you to assign multiple channel mutes to a single button. So if you want to mute all the band channels before the pastor gets up there to speak you can assign all the instrument channels to one mute group and then mute all of the channels with the push of a single button. See, sound is so easy!

## TALKBACK MIC

Allows you to connect a mic a talk to the stage mixes or address the house mix for a public announcement. These are VERY helpful and should be used instead of trying to yell over a practicing worship team. No one likes being yelled at, even if your intentions are innocent, use the talkback and keep the peace, along with saving your voice.

## AUX SENDS MASTER

For every aux send your console is equipped with you will have a master knob for the send. This is very helpful with making changes to the whole mix

## HEADPHONE LEVEL

A knob that allows you to change the volume going to your headphones. Every sound booth should have a pair of fully functional over-the-ear headphones. They are critical in so many ways (troubleshooting, cue-ing tracks, finding out who is singing a half-step flat, etc.).  When I run sound I always make sure to bring a pair of headphones with me.

## MATRIX SENDS

Not every board is equipped with these, but they are additional outputs from your subgroups or main mix to be used as needed. Some people use these to feed hearing-assistance wireless units, foyers, crying baby rooms, etc.

## MUTE GROUP MASTER

The Master buttons to mute or un-mute your mute groups

## STEREO RETURNS

Additional inputs to the console for Line-Level devices. Saves you from having to take up an entire channel for a simple input (background music from an mp3 player, etc.)

## SUB-GROUP FADERS

Controls the level of the subgroup being sent to the main output.

## SUB-GROUP ASSIGNMENT BUTTONS

In order to hear your subgroup through the house mix you must assign the group to the main L/R mix or else you will not hear it in the house!

## MAIN FADERS

Master volume control for the send to you house mix .

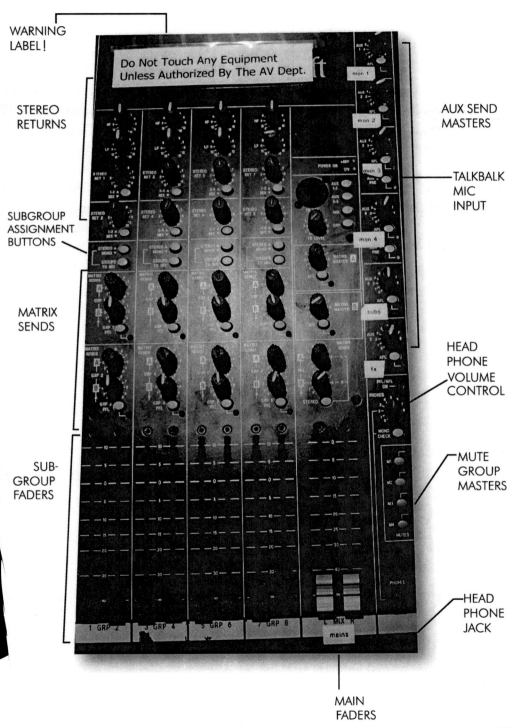

WARNING LABEL!

Do Not Touch Any Equipment Unless Authorized By The AV Dept.

STEREO RETURNS

SUBGROUP ASSIGNMENT BUTTONS

MATRIX SENDS

SUB-GROUP FADERS

AUX SEND MASTERS

TALKBALK MIC INPUT

HEAD PHONE VOLUME CONTROL

MUTE GROUP MASTERS

HEAD PHONE JACK

MAIN FADERS

45

# *Conclusion*

There's the nitty gritty of console terminology.

The first thing I do when encountering a console I have never used before is scan the layout, see where everything is placed, and then inspect channel 1. Once I am familiar with channel 1, I know the others are going to be the same, so I'm ready to work.

I know it's not fun to hear, but since every console is different it really pays to read through the owner's manual. If the manual is unavailable, just do a web search for the make and model of the console. Most manufacturers have their manuals available online for free as PDF files. Besides getting a good grasp of the unit itself, you will probably come across some new features you didn't even know were there!

# NOTES

# Section 5.

PRACTICAL SOUND ENGINEERING

Ok, now that you have the system up and running, let's make things good! The goal isn't simply to make the system work (while that is an absolute necessity), but our intention should be to make it the best we can, so this chapter will focus on the practicalities of running a distraction-free service, from set-up to tear-down.

## KEY TERMS

Stage Plot

Input List

Upstage

Downstage

Center stage

Stage Left

Stage Right

Line Check

Sound Check

Gaff Tape

# PRACTICAL SOUND ENGINEERING

- To do the job right, a sound person must be attentive, always thinking ahead, a problem solver, taking care of problems before they happen, and resolving them quickly if they do happen. A sound person must be able to work well with musicians, putting yourself in their shoes and seeing things from the musician's perspective, always doing your best to be a blessing to the musician and in turn a blessing to all the people in the audience. Sounds simple enough right?

- Making this happen is not rocket science, but it does take an important, and all too-often overlooked element: planning. Planning is not a sin. In the church we all want to be led and directed by the Holy Spirit and planning can often be seen as not being open or led by the Spirit, but this is wrong. God designed us with brains that can think ahead, and as faithful stewards of our brains, we better use them! The real problem is the result of not asking the Holy Spirit to direct us in our planning and in our preparation. We need to fully rely on the Spirit in all aspects of ministry, from the planning to the actual implementation itself.

---

These are all opportunities for worship, I can worship God as I plan, I can worship God as I set up, I can worship God as I sound check, as Paul says in 1 Corinthians 10:31 : "Whatever you do, do all things for the glory of God"!

---

## THE STAGE PLOT AND INPUT LIST

Two things that require some planning and forethought, but can reap great benefits are the STAGE PLOT and INPUT LIST. Nothing helps stage setup and soundcheck go smoother than having a stage plot and input list (although coffee can be a big help as well).

### STAGE PLOT

**A graphic displaying all the necessary stage elements for a performance and their specific location on the stage.** The stage plot can be as specific as you would like it to be, just be sure it is easy to read and and can be clearly understood without verbal explanation. Show what you need and what channel any mics or DI's should be plugged into. Don't forget essential (and often over-looked) items like power outlets or even guitar stands. Adding the name of who is standing where also increases the communication dynamics between the booth and stage.

### INPUT LIST

**A spreadsheet displaying what channel each input from the stage is connected to on the snake and on the mixing console.** The input list can also include more detailed information, like the preferred type of microphone, DI, mic stand, or processing to be used, and if phantom power is required for the channel. You can also designate if you want certain channels grouped together in a subgroup. That's a lot of information packed into one spreadsheet. That's why these are so helpful!

Below is an example stage plot and corresponding Input List:

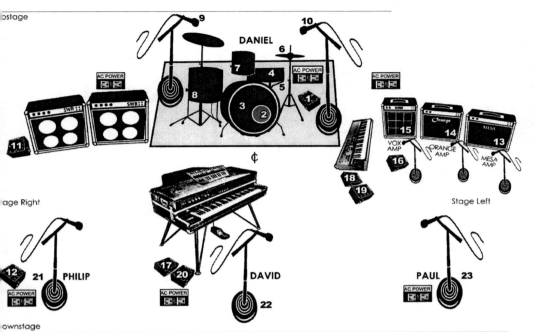

| Channel # | +48v | Input | Mic / DI | Stand | Processing | VCA |
|---|---|---|---|---|---|---|
| 1 | | Click | DI | None | | |
| 2 | * | Kick IN | Beta 91 | None | Gate / Comp. | 1 |
| 3 | | Kick OUT | D6 | Short Boom | Gate / Comp. | 1 |
| 4 | | Snare TOP | SM57 | Short Boom | Gate / Comp. | 1 |
| 5 | * | Snare BOTTOM | SM81 | Short Boom | Comp. | 1 |
| 6 | * | Hi-Hat | SM81 | Short Boom | | 1 |
| 7 | * | Rack Tom | D2/Beta 98 | Claw | Gate / Comp. | 1 |
| 8 | * | Floor Tom | D4/Beta 98 | Claw | Gate / Comp. | 1 |
| 9 | * | FOH OH L | KSM32 | Tall Boom | | 1 |
| 10 | * | FOH OH R | KSM32 | Tall Boom | | 1 |
| 11 | | Bass Line | DI | None | Comp. | 2 |
| 12 | | Bass Line (SansAmp) | DI | None | Comp. | 2 |
| 13 | | SL EG L (Mesa Amp) | SM57 | Short Boom | Comp. | 3 |
| 14 | | SL EG R (Orange Amp) | SM57 | Short Boom | Comp. | 3 |
| 15 | | EG L (Vox Amp) | SM57 | Short Boom | Comp. | 3 |
| 16 | | EG R (D.I.) | DI | None | | 3 |
| 17 | | Keys | DI | None | | 4 |
| 18 | | Korg L | Beta58 | None | | 5 |
| 19 | | Korg R | Beta58 | None | | 5 |
| 20 | | Synth | DI | None | | 5 |
| 21 | | SR Vocal | Beta58 | Tall Boom | Comp. | 6 |
| 22 | | CNTR Vocal | Beta58 | Tall Boom | Comp. | 7 |
| 23 | | SL Vocal | Beta58 | Tall Boom | Comp. | 6 |

# PRACTICAL SOUND ENGINEERING

## STAGE LOCATION

It's good to know how to describe where something is on stage and there are standardized words for this. If you look at the stage plot on the previous page you will see locations marked as: STAGE RIGHT, STAGE LEFT, UPSTAGE and DOWNSTAGE. Remember these names correspond to if you are standing on stage facing the audience. So these locations are the opposite of what you would see from the FOH position. Here's a quick chart so you can know these locations well:

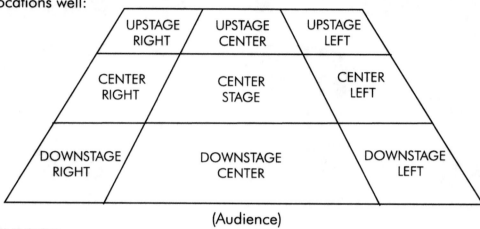

(Audience)

## UNLOCK

Why UPSTAGE and DOWNSTAGE? In the 19th century, stages were sloped, the back of the stage was higher than the front, so the rear of the stage was UP and the front of the stage was DOWN.

## THE SOUNDCHECK-CHECKLIST
**The following is a list of reminders in regards to service flow:**

1.) **Set the stage:** Follow the Stage Plot and Input List
Think what you would want (or not want) on stage if you were playing up there. Keep cables and equipment tidy and organized. No Spaghetti & No trip hazards! Keep any excess cable slack neatly coiled at the base of the mic stand or monitor, NOT AT THE STAGE-BOX. That way if a mic stand or monitor needs to be moved, you have the slack there to do it, and it prevents cable spaghetti at the stage box.

2.) **Line Check:** Have a helper speak into every mic ("Check one two") and test all connections to make sure they are correct and working BEFORE the musicians arrive. NEVER assume it will work! Always check the pastors' mic/pulpit mic beforehand. Make sure all wireless mics have fresh batteries.

1.)  **Gain Structure:** SOOO important! Keep in mind that your gain setting affects the signal for the entire channel strip, so any changes to the gain will also affect the levels of your stage mixes, main mixes, or any other send from your channel. Be sure to set it right the first time!

I once had a church call me to help them with a multitude of sound issues they were dealing with. Long story short, 90% of their sound issues were because their sound tech, despite running sound at their church for over 15 years, never touched the gain knobs! You need to set the gain afresh every sound check!

## HAVE THE MUSICIANS REALLY SING
## (Not just say "check one two") while you:

1.) Turn the Gain all the way down
2.) Un-mute the channel
3.) Bring the Fader Up to Zero (Unity)
4.) Turn the Gain up to where the signal peaks are just below zero (leave enough headroom so that if the signal gets loud for a second it won't clip the channel and distort)
5.) Repeat for every channel input that is being used

## STAGE MIX
Make sure everyone on stage has what they need to play "In Tune & In Time" and that they are comfortable and free to play without worrying about the mix. Keep good eye contact with the band throughout sound-check and the set to make sure they aren't gesturing for any changes to their mix.

## HOUSE MIX
Put every sound in its proper sonic place (always keeping the lead vocals on top of the mix). Keep the mix alive, don't just walk away once the band gets started. **Always ask yourself "How can this mix be better?"** and resolve the weak areas in the mix.

## GOING "LIVE"
As the service begins, be alert and **always be thinking two steps ahead.** Remember: The key is to be distraction free! So what is going to happen next? Be ready so that transitions can be smooth and seamless. Is the pastor walking up to the pulpit? Have his mic channel unmuted and ready to go. Avoid the "is this thing on?... can you hear me out there?" type of distractions. Is a guitar player about to unplug his guitar? Mute the channel before he unplugs to avoid the "pop" explosion that will startle everyone and could quench the Spirit after a sweet time of worship!

## STRIKING STAGE
When the service is done. Break it all down and roll the cables up properly to keep the gear working for the long-term. Use the "under over" method of rolling cable. Keep mic clips with mics and not on mic stands to prevent broken or missing clips. Keep all of your equipment labeled and organized.

# PRACTICAL SOUND ENGINEERING

## POWER DOWN
Power down the system properly. (See the section on Amps and Speakers)

## OTHER KEY AREA"S OF "KNOW HOW"

### 1.) Troubleshooting:
When something goes wrong, stay calm, think logically, follow the signal path and remember: The output of one device is the input of the next device. So if a microphone isn't working, but you are getting signal at the console, you can rule out a bad cable, a bad mic, a bad snake, etc. You probably have a routing issue at the console, or it's probably that the phantom power isn't on!! It's usually something simple so don't panic.

### 2.) Equipment Maintenance:
- Cable Tips: Buy good cables, Label the cables, Use shorter cables when possible. Have a cable tester at the ready. Always cross audio and AC (power) cables at a 90° angle when possible.

- Be sure to properly loosen mic stands before adjusting them or breaking them down. If the stand is forced closed the internal bolt will strip, making the stand weak, unstable, and unusable.

-When taping down cable, never use duct tape. Always have Gaffer's tape handy and be sure to use it.

## UNLOCK
GAFFER'S Tape (aka Gaff Tape) is a cloth-based tape designed for securing cables to the floor. It is durable yet easy to tear and the best thing is that it will not leave sticky residue on the cables or on the floor. It is more expensive than other common tapes, (like duct tape), but is a necessary tool in live audio. Never, I repeat, never use duct tape for securing cables to the floor or anything else, it will end up costing you more in the long run because you'll need new cables and new carpet!

## KEEP YOUR GEAR CLEAN AND DRY
Two things that will damage audio gear:

1)**Liquids:** So keep drinks away from the console!

2) **Dust.** So keep your equipment clean and maintained! A small, unused paintbrush works great for dusting in between all the knobs of equipment. Compressed air, Deoxidizing spray, contact cleaner are helpful for keeping your jacks and pots smooth and free of "crackle."

## FEEDBACK: THE ENEMY OF AUDIO
When it comes to distractions caused by the sound system, there is no greater culprit than FEEDBACK. What is feedback? Feedback refers to the loop that is created when the amplified output of the speakers becomes the input of the microphone and thus becomes re-amplified again...and again...and again until the unmistakable squealing occurs.

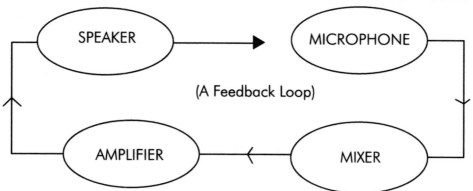

(A Feedback Loop)

This re-amplification can happen in a split second and usually occurs at the worst time, like during an intimate prayer. So how can we eliminate feedback when it occurs and prevent it from occurring again?

### HOW TO ELIMINATE AND PREVENT FEEDBACK

Immediate fix = Turn it down!!
If feedback begins, your knee-jerk reaction should be to turn down the channel that is causing it.
**The Catch 22** - Your mic is feeding back so you turn it down, but now it is too quiet and people can no longer hear it in the house, so you turn it up, but then it starts feeding back again! What do you do? Try the following:

### ADJUST GAIN

Having a proper gain setting is critical for preventing feedback. If your gain is too high the microphone will be increasingly sensitive and more prone to receiving its own sound waves coming from the loudspeakers.

### EQ

Oftentimes it's not the entire signal that is feeding back, but rather certain frequencies. This is the difference between a squealing feedback (high frequency) and a rumbling feedback (low frequency). Using your EQ controls, you must find the troublesome frequency and turn it down. This allows you to only turn down the feedback frequency without having to decrease the volume of the entire channel.

### SPEAKER/MIC PLACEMENT

Speaker/Mic Placement: Sometimes moving some things around on stage best solves the problem. First, **having a microphone in front of the house speakers is to be avoided at all costs.** I have seen people place their main speakers on speaker-stands behind the band because it's more space-efficient or is more aesthetically pleasing. This will lead to feedback issues all day long and ends up making the sound a nightmare for everyone, so always keep your main loudspeakers out in front of the stage.

Secondly, it's very easy to create a feedback loop when you have a floor monitor pointed directly at a microphone (another reason why IEM's are helpful). But microphones have an area of rejection, (see "Polar Patterns" in the microphones section) so the floor wedge MUST BE AIMED AT THE AREA OF REJECTION. For cardiod mics that means the monitor must be aiming the sound waves at the back of the mic, not the front or sides, but a super-cardiod or hyper-cardiod would receive sound from the back and must be aimed at an angle from the side of the microphone.

## TUNE THE ROOM:

Sometimes a room has a particular frequency that is especially troublesome, this is where your main EQ comes to the rescue. Using RTA (Real-Time Analysis) software and an RTA microphone, you can determine if your room and system have some troublesome frequencies and then using your main EQ, turn those particular frequencies down. This process is sometimes referred to as "Tuning the Room" or "Pinking the Room" because of the pink-noise that is used for the RTA process.

# *Conclusion*

There are so many small details that must all come together for the distraction-free service to happen. All it takes is for a single unforeseen event to occur (like a battery going dead) and a chain reaction can start to take place that leads to a train wreck of a service. The more planning and preparation that has gone into the service beforehand, the more on top of things you can be so that when the unforeseen occurs, you can be ready and flexible, knowing that the other details are already under control.

# NOTES

# *Section 6.*

## MICROPHONES

Microphones are the ears of our audio system. They simply take sound waves and convert them to electricity. Mics come in all shapes and sizes, and they are the most popular piece of audio gear in the world, but alas, all microphones are not created equal; in fact, no two microphones are exactly identical. So what are we to do? Keep calm and read on

## KEY TERMS

Dynamic

Condenser

Polar Pattern

Cardiod

Proximity Effect

On-Axis

Off-Axis

3-to-1 Rule

# MICROPHONES

There are two key distinguishing factors between microphones:
1.) TYPE of microphone
2.) POLAR PATTERN of the microphone

Let's start with microphone TYPES: As I've stated a couple of times now, a microphone simply converts acoustic sound wave energy into electrical energy, but there are different methods by which to make this conversion happen. So when I say there are different TYPES of microphones, it means that there are different ways by which to convert the acoustic sound wave into an electrical current and the way by which you convert the sound will have an effect on the way it sounds and the application of the mic.

## UNLOCK

The technical term for a device that converts energy from one form to another is a TRANSDUCER, and that's what a microphone is, a transducer. Loudspeakers are also transducers, converting electrical energy into acoustic sound energy.

### There are two primary TYPES of microphones:

### DYNAMIC Microphone:

A dynamic mic uses a magnetic coil conversion, what that means for you is that the microphone can withstand high SPL's without distorting. So these types of mics are great for kick drums, snare drums, guitar amps, and they sound good on vocals too. Dynamic mics are also designed to be fairly rugged and able to withstand some of the abuse that comes with the live sound environment (like lead singers using the mic as a drumstick). The industry standard mics of this type are the Shure SM57 (designed for instrument use) and SM58 (designed for use with vocals). Both of these mics are used worldwide and have proven themselves to be reliable workhorses. There are many other great options out there as well, from a multitude of brands like Sennheiser, Audix, Audio Technica, AKG, and Heil.

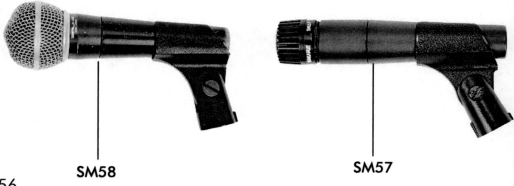

SM58                                    SM57

### CONDENSER MICHROPHONE:

A condenser mic (sometimes referred to as a "capacitor" mic) uses a floating diaphragm conversion process. The key points to remember with a condenser mic is that:

1. They require PHANTOM POWER (aka " +48v ") in order to function. It's very important to remember this because if you don't have phantom power activated on the channel the condenser microphone WILL NOT WORK. If troubleshooting a dead condenser mic, the first thing to check is if the phantom power is on, cause 90% of the time this is the problem!

**UNLOCK** ———————————————————————

PHANTOM POWER is a charge that runs backwards, from the sound board to the microphone, via the same XLR cable that the microphone uses to send signal to the board. It might seem crazy that power can run over the same cable that also has an audio signal running through it, but it works so flawlessly that it is indistinguishable (hence the name "phantom power"!). The phantom voltage can range anywhere from 12 to 52 volts, but 48volts is most commonly used, hence the "48v" button on most consoles. ————————————

2. They are more sensitive than a Dynamic Mic. This is a good and bad thing. It's good because they generally have a wider frequency range than a dynamic mic, especially in the highs. Since condensers are better at picking up high frequencies it makes them better on cymbals, some stringed instruments, and some vocals as well. The sensitivity is bad when it comes to high SPL's. Condensers can't handle loud sound waves as well as dynamic mics can, so they don't work well on kick or snare drums, but some condensers are equipped with a PAD switch that basically attenuates (aka turns down) the signal and makes them more functional with high SPL's.

3. They can be very small. The design of a condenser allows for it to be made in many different sizes, from the tiny lavalier (aka "lapel") mic to the large-diaphragm condenser found in recording studios. In the church we usually don't like the pastor's face hidden behind some massive microphone, so we often use condenser mics due to the fact that they can be nearly invisible (like the Countryman E6i headset mic).

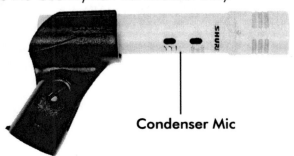

**Condenser Mic**

# MICROPHONES

Note that there are other types of microphones (like Ribbon mics), but the Dynamic and Condenser are the most common. Below is a chart with recommended uses for the two different types of microphones.

## SUGGESTED MICROPHONE USE:

| DYNAMIC MICS | CONDENSER MICS |
|---|---|
| Kick Drum | Hi Hat, Cymbals |
| Snare Drum | Light Percussion (Shakers) |
| Toms | Piano/Strings |
| Guitar Amps | Choir |
| Percussion: Djembe, Cajon | Ambient or "Room" Mics |
| Vocals | Vocals |

**Note:** The placement of the microphone in relation to the sound source will have a great affect on the tone that comes from the microphone.

### Now let's discus MICROPHONE POLARITY

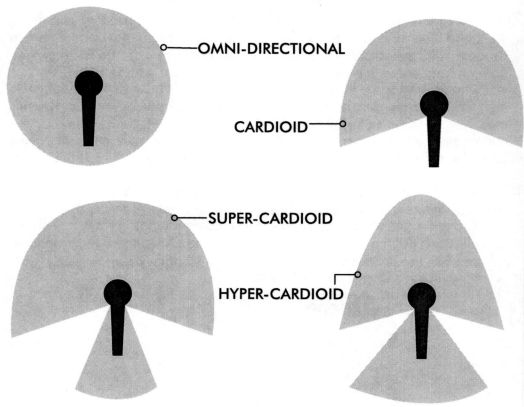

OMNI-DIRECTIONAL

CARDIOID

SUPER-CARDIOID

HYPER-CARDIOID

## BIDIRECTIONAL

Every microphone, no matter what type it is, has a POLAR PATTERN. A polar pattern represents the direction from where the microphone is designed to receive sound. Microphones are designed to receive sound waves from certain directions and reject sound waves from other directions. This is extremely useful for us sound engineers and we can really use polar patterns to our advantage in both feedback rejection and avoiding microphone bleed.

## UNLOCK

MICROPHONE BLEED is when other sound sources from the stage "spill over" into a microphone directed at a different sound source. A common example of this is when a vocal microphone also picks up the sound waves coming from the drums. The problem with bleed is that when you turn up the vocals in the mix you consequently turn up the drums as well.

## OMNI-DIRECTIONAL

Picks up sound waves equally from all directions. These would be impossible to use for a vocalist on stage with a stage wedge because it would be feeding back like crazy. But omni-directional mics exhibit no proximity effect, so they can be useful for head-set mics and lapel mics.

## UNLOCK

**What is Proximity Effect?** The closer you get to a sound source with a directional mic, the louder the bass response will be, this is known as proximity effect. So if a singer wants a bassier (or "warmer") tone they should sing closer to the mic, if they want to clear the tone up a bit, they should back away from the mic an inch or so (to taste). This is also true for mic'ing guitar cabinets or any other instrument or sound source. If it's a directional mic (like a cardiod), you'll have proximity effect, so be aware of it, and use it to your advantage when necessary.

### BI-DIRECTIONAL
Picks up sound equally from the front and the back. We don't see these on the live stage very much, but are more common in recording studio applications.

### CARDIOID
By far the most popular polar pattern (it's what is used on the SM57's and SM58's), it picks up sound from the front of the mic and not from the back. Perfect for when you have a stage wedge pointed directly up at the back of a mic.

### SUPER AND HYPER CARDIOID
These two patterns are similar, but not exactly the same thing. Both of them are designed to have a tighter pattern than a standard cardiod for pickup in the front. Since the pattern isn't as wide as a cardiod, it focuses in on the sound source directly in front, which helps to reduce the bleed from other sound sources. The only downside is that while the pattern is tighter in the front, they don't reject sound as well from the back.

This is VERY important to note, because with a cardiod mic you would want to place the monitor wedge directly (180°) behind the mic, but with the super or hyper cardiod you DO NOT want to do that, instead you would want to place the monitor at an angle: 125° for supercardiod and 110° for hypercardiod. This simple adjustment to the placement of monitors can be extremely effective in feedback rejection, thus allowing you to get the monitors louder if necessary.

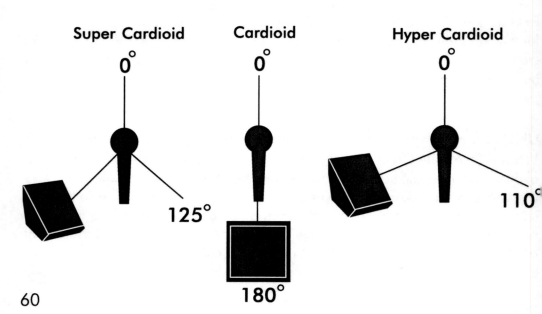

**Super Cardioid** 0°   **Cardioid** 0°   **Hyper Cardioid** 0°

125°   180°   110°

**UNLOCK**

So what's the difference between super-cardiod and hyper-cardiod? I boil it down like this: both patterns are tighter in the front area than a standard cardiod, but **a hyper is tighter in the front than a super.** Both patterns have less rejection in the rear than a standard cardiod, but **a super has more rear rejection than a hyper.** So they are similar, but not identical.

Every microphone will have these two fundamental characteristics, its TYPE and its PATTERN. Knowing these two facts for every microphone you use helps you to both apply them wisely and use them creatively.

**The #1 Rule with Sound:** Here it is, the secret tip you have been waiting for to solve all of your sound difficulties. The #1 rule with sound is that THERE ARE NO RULES! Yes, that's too simple I know, but as you learn some of the technicalities behind sound and its equipment, remember it all boils down to just making it sound good. So I may give you guidelines (like what mic type to use on certain instruments), these aren't hard fast rules, they are recommendations from experience, but you can always try something different, if it doesn't distract and it sounds awesome, then perfect, go with it!

## MICROPHONE TECHNIQUE

Now that you know a bit about the function of the microphone, it is good to know some microphone technique. Where you place a microphone (where it is "aimed") will have a significant influence on the sound itself. Knowing some basic microphone technique can help you shape the tone of a sound before you even touch the EQ controls on your board. Hearing the difference between one mic position and the next requires focused listening, so a sound engineer must learn to listen closely and actively, not be flippant or passive in your listening.

**What plays into microphone technique?** Knowing the type and pattern of the mic is a good start, but also knowing a little about the instrument or sound source will prove helpful as well. Where are the sound waves primarily coming from? Pointing the mic directly at the location where sound waves are projecting will sound very different than from where they are not. For instance, on an acoustic guitar the sound waves project from the sound hole on the body of the guitar. Pointing a mic directly at the sound hole will produce a very different tone than if you place the mic directly in front of the 12th fret of the neck. Don't believe me? Try it, listen, then tell all of your friends about the new sound trick you just learned. You'll hear that when you mic the sound hole you get a lot of "boomy-ness" whereas at the 12th fret it will be more thin and clear.

# MICROPHONES

## UNLOCK

When you point a microphone directly at the location where the sound waves project it is referred to as ON AXIS mic placement whereas pointing it in an indirect location it is called OFF AXIS mic placement.

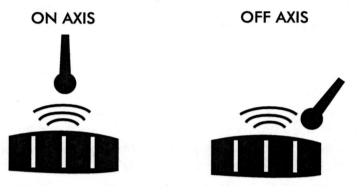

**ON AXIS**　　　　　　　　　　**OFF AXIS**

**As a final test to our introduction** to mic technique, let's look at the mic placement for an electric guitar. First, where does the sound come from? It comes from a speaker (or speakers) in a speaker cabinet connected to the electric guitar amp. So step 1, mic the speaker! This might seem obvious, but since the speaker is usually hidden behind some cloth called a SPEAKER GRILL it is not always exactly clear where the speaker is. If I had a dollar for every time I've caught a sound person just slapping a mic on a cabinet without checking to see if the mic is even pointing at a speaker I'd have at least $15!

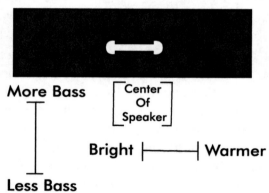

**More Bass** | Center Of Speaker

Bright ├────┤ Warmer

**Less Bass**

**Getting the mic directed at a speaker is only Step One:** when placing a mic on a guitar amp we must also remember PROXIMITY EFFECT. Assuming you are using a directional mic (and you probably are), the closer the mic is to the speaker will result in more bass in the overall tone. Too bassy? Scoot the mic back an inch, and adjust to taste. (Another benefit with close-mic'ing a sound as opposed to further away is that you can get more of the direct sound source and less bleed). We must also remember ON AXIS vs. OFF AXIS.

With a speaker, on axis mic placement would be pointing the mic directly at the center of the speaker and this would result in a brighter, and more crisp sound. Off axis, on the other hand, is placing the mic off-center, resulting in a warmer tone. Whereas off axis would be considered placing the mic off-center and would result in a warmer tone. So you have both your PROXIMITY and AXIS to consider. You, of course, should add in your knowledge of microphone TYPES as well, knowing that a condenser will give you more highs, but might not be able to get as close to the speaker due to SPL's whereas a dynamic mic will allow you to get right up on the speaker grill, but might roll off the highs at 15k. Remember, there are no rules. Take your knowledge, use your ears, create a good mix. (All that to say, I love the sound of an SM57 on an electric guitar amp, so start there!)

## WHAT ABOUT MIC TECHNIQUE WITH MULTIPLE MICS?

When you have multiple mics near each other on stage (where the same sound wave can be picked up by both mics but at different distances) you risk signal degradation or total phase cancellation. The result is referred to as COMB FILTERING, where different frequencies in the audio signal are being cancelled out, making your signal sound weak, thin, and probably just weird (no description of roadies intended).

**So what can you do?  The solution is THE 3:1 RULE**. Yes, there are no rules with sound…except this one. The 3:1 rule states: To avoid phase issues between two microphones, ensure that microphone B is placed at least 3 times as far away from microphone A, as microphone A is from the sound source. So if the closest mic is 1 foot from the sound source the second mic needs to be at least 3 feet from the other mic.

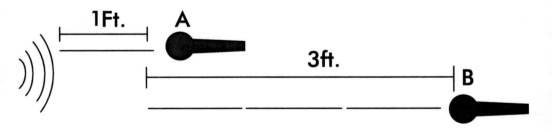

# *Conclusion* ────────────────────────────○

I know that setting up, line checking, sound checking, and mixing a band is a time consuming process that takes a lot of mental energy, but never forget the most important microphone on the platform: the pastor's mic. With any public speaking you want to ensure vocal intelligibility, that everyone can hear clearly so that each word is understandable. But in a church it is paramount. Remember, faith comes by hearing, and hearing by the word of God (Romans 10:17). I would hope and pray that while your worship team is leading songs that are theologically sound and Biblically rich in content, your pastor would also be bringing the word of God.

We know from both Romans 12 and 1 Corinthians 12 that God has appointed people in each church body to be teachers, and as Paul writes to Timothy in 2 Timothy 4:2, these men should be faithful to "preach the word." These pastors have been given a charge to speak the word of God so that people may hear it, come to faith in Christ, and through the continued hearing of the word, grow in their faith that they may walk by it and not by sight. (2 Corinthians 5:7). So then, it is our primary duty in this ministry of sound, to ensure that the word can be heard!

This means that even in the busyness of set up and sound check, planning and time is given to test and dial-in the pastor's mic. Don't let it be an afterthought, make it primary. If he's using a wireless mic, make sure the batteries are fresh and working. Don't gamble with the, "I think there's enough battery life to make it through the sermon" mentality. Having a mic cut out, feedback, or fall off in the middle of the service is a distraction that should have been avoided if given the proper planning and prioritizing. **As an audio engineer in the church, there is no greater service you can give the people of your congregation than to faithfully facilitate the hearing of God's word.**

# NOTES

# Section 7.

===

## AMPS AND SPEAKERS

We have reached the end of our signal path, or have we? Yes, we have. This is final big push that the audio needs to reach our listener's ears.

### KEY TERMS

Amplifier

Tweeter

Mid-Range Driver

Woofer

Crossover

Subwoofer

# AMPS AND SPEAKERS

In the blink of an eye, our sound has traveled a long distance, been through a lot of processing, and has now arrived at the final leg of the journey: The amplifier and speakers.

An amplifier (or "amp" for short) is a device that increases the power of a signal. What's coming out of an amplifier is an exact replica of what goes into an amplifier, only bigger!

**Remember, there are some variations in where your amps might be located:**
When an amp is built into a mixing board, it is called a powered mixer
When an amp is built into a speaker, it is called a powered speaker.
There are pros and cons to each of these devices, but manufacturers give you options in what to purchase so that you can get what suits your situation best.

Believe it or not, there is a right and wrong way to turn a sound system off and on. The key point to remember is that to avoid possibly damaging your system, **you always want your amps off when other devices are being turned off or on.**
So, when you power up a sound system the amps should be turned on LAST.
And when you power down a system the amps should be turned off FIRST.

### Matching the amps to the speakers:
Always be sure your amps and speakers are well suited for each other in both wattage and impedance. One big advantage of powered speakers is that you know the amp and speakers are designed for each other.

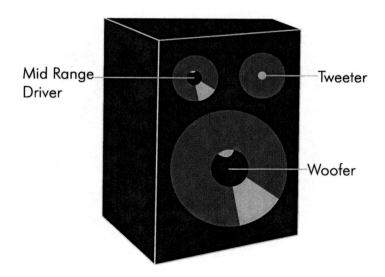

Mid Range Driver

Tweeter

Woofer

## WHAT IS A SPEAKER?

A speaker (or more specifically:"loudspeaker") is an actually a transducer (just like a microphone, but with the opposite function) that converts electrical energy into an acoustic sound wave. The word "Speaker" is actually a somewhat vague term. Engineers discovered many years ago that speakers could obtain higher fidelity and efficiency if they didn't have to replicate the entire 20hz to 20kHz audio spectrum.

Instead the spectrum should be split up into separate sections and each section can have its own loudspeaker "driver" that is designed specifically to replicate sound waves in that frequency section.  So what we usually refer to as a "speaker" is specifically a wooden cabinet that houses separate audio drivers. A standard enclosure can contain 3 separate drivers:

      Tweeter = Replicates High Frequencies
      Mid Range Driver = Replicates Mid-range frequencies
      Woofer = Replicates Low Frequencies

How does the audio signal get split into its different frequency sections and sent to its specific driver? A device called a CROSSOVER does that. There are two types: ACTIVE and PASSIVE. You never see a passive crossover because they are built into the speaker cabinet itself and the frequency cutoff points are preset. Active crossovers are external units placed before the amps in the signal path, allowing the user to set the exact frequency points (aka CROSSOVER FREQUENCIES) at which you want to split the signal.

### SUBS

In modern music, no speaker gets as much attention as the subwoofer. The SUB-WOOFER (or "SUB") is a speaker driver designed specifically to replicate sound waves below 100Hz. This driver has the smallest frequency range to cover, but the largest sound waves to reproduce, which is why they are generally large drivers, ranging in size from 8-inches to 34-inches! Our bodies can tell if the subwoofer is working or not (we feel sound waves that low) and if you want a system that can give you the full audio spectrum you will need subwoofers.

### THE AUX FED SUB

I prefer to connect my subs via a post fader aux send on my console instead of sending my entire house mix to the sub. This gives me more specific control over what is being sent to the subs (usually just kick, bass, and the occasional floor tom and synth)

# Conclusion

Now that you know about the parts of a speaker, remember this: KEEP THE SPEAKERS DIRECTED AT THE LISTENERS' EARS. I have seen speakers aimed at people's shins, over people's heads, pointed at a wall, all sorts of crazy stuff. There is no magnetic forcefield that pulls sound waves into our ears, so we need to be sure that we are aiming our speaker cabinets so that the sound waves leaving them are going DIRECTLY to the ears of our listeners, not bouncing off of walls. Direct sound will give the listener clarity, and we like clarity in our mixes!

# NOTES

# *Section 8.*

═══════════════
═══════════════

## CHANGING THE TONE

Equalization can be a sound person's best friend. It is the tool we use like a sculptor's chisel to refine and shape the sound, so we must know how to best wield our chisel!

## KEY TERMS

Equalization

Graphic EQ

Parametric EQ

Linear EQ

Q

Shelf EQ

# CHANGING THE TONE

A sound system in its most basic form will amplify the signals from stage, but that's not all it can do. We also have a very powerful tool at our fingertips that allows us to actually shape the way something sounds. This tool is Equalization (aka EQ). **EQ allows you to boost or cut frequencies in any part of the audio spectrum (remember, 20Hz-20kHz) to achieve a desired tone.** Does something sound too thick, too thin, or is it getting lost in the mix due to lack of clarity? Well EQ is your tool to refine the sound and shape so it sits in its proper place in the mix. EQ is everywhere, but it can look different. This is because there are different types, they are:

## GRAPHIC:

Usually a rack mounted device with many small faders. Each fader controls the amplitude of a preset frequency, oftentimes referred to as a "band". So a "31-band graphic EQ" (like the one seen below) is a unit that has 31 pre-selected frequencies that you can either boost (turn up, "amplify") or cut (turn down, attenuate) to your liking.

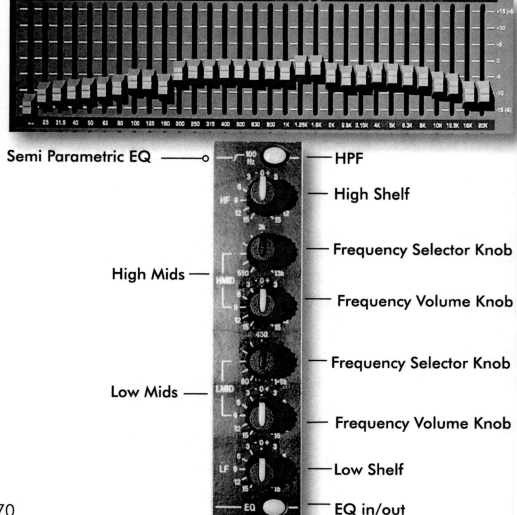

Semi Parametric EQ ——o —— HPF

High Shelf

Frequency Selector Knob

High Mids —— Frequency Volume Knob

Frequency Selector Knob

Low Mids —— Frequency Volume Knob

Low Shelf

EQ in/out

## PARAMETRIC:

Found on the channels strips of most mixing consoles, this type of EQ uses not just one knob, but two! One knob is a frequency selector, used for selecting the specific frequency (Hz) you want to adjust. The other knob is a volume knob (dB), it allows you to either turn up or turn down the frequency you selected with the first knob. Parametric EQ doesn't have a preset frequency like a graphic EQ; it gives you the control by allowing you to do the selecting.

**UNLOCK**

Some consoles will boast of "Fully Parametric EQ", while others will say they have "Semi-Parametric" EQ. The difference between these two is the Q control. When we adjust a frequency with our EQ controls it's important to note that we aren't just affecting that single frequency, we're also the affecting the frequencies neighboring that "center" frequency. How many neighboring frequencies do we affect? That depends on the width of your EQ bands (aka the "bandwidth"). Q is a bandwidth control, it allows you to select how wide or narrow your EQ bell curve will be, thus affecting how many other frequencies you will adjust.

**The Q knob** on a fully parametric console will generally show Q settings in a numeric value. Know that a high numeric value for Q (like 8.6) equates to a very narrow bandwidth and a low value (like .7) equates to a wide bandwidth. High Q settings are useful in removing a troublesome frequency with surgical accuracy, but lower Q settings are generally more gentle and natural sounding.

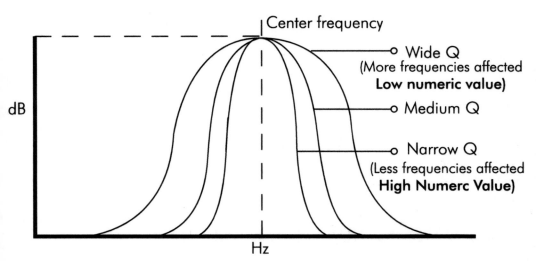

## LINEAR:

Found on digital boards, recording software, and tablet console controllers, linear EQ is a visual depiction of an EQ curve that allows you to see the line of your EQ curve on a display screen. These are generally parametric EQ's in an easy-to-see layout.

### Linear EQ Showing a High Shelf, Low Shelf, and Mid-range Boost

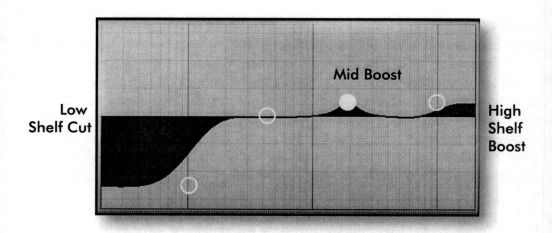

My Board just has a knob for "Hi" and a knob for "Lo."

There is a type of EQ called Shelving EQ or a "Shelf". A shelf can be used on the high end of the audio spectrum or the low end (A High Shelf or Low Shelf) and has one selected frequency. When you choose to boost or cut the frequency you will also boost all the frequencies ABOVE (on a high shelf) and all the frequencies BELOW (on a low shelf). For instance, if the EQ on the channel strip of my console just has a single pot for the highs, I know that if I boost that knob I will be boosting the frequency (usually around 12kHz) and all the frequencies above 12k.

### Subtractive EQ:

Oftentimes live sound engineers prefer to use Subtractive EQ, which involves turning frequencies down instead of boosting frequencies. This is helpful when feedback is an issue, as boosting frequencies can lead to feedback in those frequency ranges, but you'll never know until you try. That's what sound check is for – dialing in the best sound you can get while no one is there. Once you've "gone live" and the service has actually begun your time for EQ experimentation is over, don't risk a distracting feedback explosion because you wanted to see what an additional 6dB of 12k would sound like on the lead vocal.

EQ Recommendations
Below is a chart showing good starting points when it comes to EQ on various sound sources. Experiment (during sound check, NOT during the service) with these settings and listen closely to how they affect the sound individually and also how changing the EQ on one sound can affect the mix as a whole.

## EQ GUIDELINES

| Instrument | Frequencies to Turn Down | Frequencies to Turn Up |
|---|---|---|
| Kick | 250Hz | 50Hz, 3-5kHZ |
| Snare | HPF | 6kHz |
| Hi Hats | HPF everything below 250Hz | 3kHz, 7-10kHz |
| High Tom | HPF | 6kHz |
| Low Tom | 200-300Hz | 50-100Hz, 5kHz |
| Overheads | HPF everything below 250Hz | 10-12kHz |
| Bass Guitar | 200-500Hz | 40-100Hz, 5kHz |
| Acoustic Guitar | HPF, 600-800Hz | 4-6kHz |
| Electric Guitar | HPF, 6-8kHz | 1-2kHz |
| Keys | 300-500Hz | 5-7kHz |
| Female Vox | HPF, 200-500Hz | 3-5kHz, 10-12kHz |
| Male Vox | HPF, 200-500Hz | 5-7kHz, 10-12kHz |

HPF = Activate the High Pass Filter (aka Low Cut)

## Conclusion

Dialing in a great sounding mix for a band is a combination of ears and understanding. Assuming the musicians are doing their part in providing you with well-played music, the sound person must do their part to combine all the audio sources from the band into a solid single mix. To do this, a sound engineer must have the understanding of: 1) the role each sound source will play in the mix, and 2) how to use the equipment to shape the sound properly. Of course all this is for naught if the sound engineer doesn't have an ear that is actively listening to the mix and assessing what needs to be adjusted to shape the mix properly. So, it's a combination of ears and understanding.

In regards to understanding the role each sound source plays in the final mix I like to think of it in terms of arranging furniture. If I'm arranging the furniture in a room I can move it all in and pile it up in the middle of the room.

## *Conclusion* (Cont.)

My couches, chairs, tables, lamps, bookshelves, rugs, everything in a massive heap and I can say, "there, I'm done, the room is finished." This is how some mixes are, yes we succeed at getting the signals from stage through to the system (like getting the furniture in the room), but nothing is in its proper place, it's just a pile of sound. Look at each sound source on stage, whether it's an instrument or a vocal and see it as a piece of furniture: what role does it play in the room? What is its purpose? Where should it therefore be located in the room to best serve its purpose? With audio we do the same: what role does this instrument play in the song? What is its purpose? Where should it go in the mix? Our ears can only hear from 20Hz to 20kHz so all the instruments must share that range, and a clear mix is a mix that doesn't just pile all the sound sources up the middle. A clear mix is one that spreads the sounds out to use the full spectrum of frequencies. If you have two electric guitars, don't have them sounding the same, emphasize a frequency on one guitar, but a different frequency on the other guitar. Sounds can complement each other, like a pair of reclining chairs, but don't stack the recliners on top of each other because it will render both chairs useless. **So think of EQ as a tool for organizing your furniture.**

# NOTES

# *Section 9.*

ARTIST'S PALETTE

There is a definite artistic side to audio. It's not merely technical all the time; once you know your tools and how to use them, you are free to sculpt and create works of art for the ears to enjoy. Like a painter has a palette of colors to choose from, the audio engineer has a variety of effects to choose from. Let's look at some of them now.

## KEY TERMS

Dynamic Range

Compressor

Reverb

Delay

Tap Tempo

# ARTIST'S PALETTE

## BEGINNING ─────────────────────────────────────o

With an almost endless number of effects (aka FX) available to us today, I like to group similar ones into families. Each effect has its own personality and function, but in the grand scheme of things some of them are very similar to each other in design and application. The first family we need to start with is by far the most practical of all the effects, the Dynamics Processors. Dynamics processors are really more of an "affect" than they are an "effect", because the basis of what they do simply affects the dynamic range of a signal, but if tweaked in extreme ways, these units can create more of an effect than simply affect.

## UNLOCK ──────────────────────────────────────🔑

**What is DYNAMIC RANGE?** Dynamic range is the difference between the quietest a signal ever gets and the loudest the signal ever gets. It deals completely with VOLUME and is measured in decibels. So if a song has a dynamic range of 70 dB it means that the loudest part of the song is 70dB louder than the quietest part in the song. **All music, from the instruments to the singers, (as well as any good public speakers) will have dynamic range,** it's actually a key element in making something interesting to listen to. Our ears would get bored listening to something at the same volume the entire time. ─────────────────────

### The Dynamics Processor family includes the:

**Compressor:** A device that reduces the overall dynamic range of a signal by reducing the volume peaks. Imagine if you could have a sound assistant whose full-time job was to turn down the fader of any channel that suddenly got too loud. In fact, this assistant would be so good that they could foresee when a signal was going to get too loud BEFORE our ears could even hear it! Well these assistants exist and they are called compressors. "Compressor" is the perfect name for this device because that is exactly what it does (and it sounds a lot better than "Compactor"), it reduces the loud peaks of a signal, thereby allowing us to turn up the overall gain of a signal and therefore making the quiet sounds louder. The quiet parts go up, the loud parts go down, and you end up with a consistent signal with no surprises.

### The Compressor and Perceived Loudness:

The compressor is helpful in many situations, but take for instance a lead vocal. When a compressor is applied to a lead vocal its dynamic range is smoothened out. No more high reaching volume peaks or soft volume valleys, just a signal that is consistent, solid, and loud. Studies have shown that our ears (and the brain attached to them) will usually focus on the loudest sound at any given time. Yes, we hear everything going on, but we really focus on whatever is loudest, so when a vocal is compressed it can impart the perception of being the loudest signal all the time, because it never gets too quiet, thus making it easier to have it sit on top of the rest of the mix.

## Limiter:

A more extreme form of compression. The limiter is like the compressor's no-nonsense older brother. If you set the limiter so that the signal won't get louder than 5dBu, then the limiter will proceed to bum rush and pounce on any signal that approaches the -5dBu threshold. Limiters are at times referred to as a "brick wall" and that is the best mental picture to have of a limiter; it simply says, "no volume peak shall pass". These can be used on vocals as well, but are also very handy on main and auxiliary outputs as a way to protect amps, speaker components, and IEM's from loud volume spikes (or feedback explosions). A limiter is a must have for the IEM signal path (and most IEM wireless units have a limiter built-in) due to the high risk of hearing damage.

## Noise Gate (or simply "gate"):

a device that works like an automatic mute switch. With a gate you can set a low threshold on the unit and say, "whenever a signal gets quieter than this threshold you can go ahead and mute the channel, but as soon as the signal gets louder than the threshold you have to un-mute the channel." This is what a gate does, it either lets the sounds through (the gate is open) or cuts the sound off (the gate is closed). This is very handy on a noisy electric guitar amp that sounds fine when the guitarist is playing, but when he stops playing all you hear is the amp buzzing. In this case, the threshold would be set just above the volume of the buzz, so when the guitarist is playing, the gate is open, but when he stops and the volume falls below the threshold, the gate closes, and signal to the channel is cut. Gates are also used on tom mics quite frequently. Since a tom drum might go a good two minutes or more in a song without ever being played, the gate can minimize the bleed coming into the tom mic from neighboring sound sources (like the kick, snare drum and hi-hats).

## Expander:

A less extreme form of a noise gate. Yes, the expander is like the noise gate's much nicer little sister. Where a noise gate would slam closed on a signal when it drops below the threshold, the expander will simply turn the signal down a bit. An expander gets its name from the fact that it actually EXPANDS the dynamic range of signal but making the quiet parts EVEN QUIETER (and it can make the loud parts even louder if you so desire), but it doesn't turn the signal all the way down like a gate would. This is useful if you want to reduce microphone bleed on channels where a gate might be too noticeable.

Now let's get into some effects that are more blatantly discernible by the listener. The first of which is the most widely used of all the FX in our arsenal: Reverb.

# ARTIST'S PALETTE

**Reverb (short for "Reverberation", it's also known as simply "verb") is the continuation of a signal after the original sound has ceased.** Sound waves can bounce off of a surface, like reflecting light off of your wristwatch into someone's eye (not that I ever did that...intentionally...during 7th grade English class) Sound waves can reflect around a room, especially if the surfaces in the room (the walls, ceilings, and floors) are hard (reflective) and not soft (absorptive)

## A Blindfold, an Empty Warehouse, and Me

Our brains love reverberation, and are quite used to hearing it constantly. If you take me blindfolded into an empty warehouse (I hope you never will), my brain will be able to perceive rather quickly that I am in a very large room. How does it do that? It's quite simple, my ears would hear the original sound wave, and then hear the reflections that traveled across the warehouse and back to my ears. My brain would use the time difference between the original sound reaching my ears and the reflections to conclude that the reflections traveled a long distance before ricocheting back to my ears, so therefore the room must be big! Our brains are doing these sub-conscious calculations all the time because we are hearing reverb all the time.

Just as the reverb in a warehouse gives us a sense of space and depth, it can do the same for our audio mixes. Sound waves that are captured by mics are usually done so within the range of a few inches, so the sound we capture is very direct, we would call this a DRY, un-reverberated signal. Imagine a microphone as an ear; if someone sang into your ear like they do a microphone we would find it very uncomfortable to say the least, we need some space! Adding reverb to the dry signals coming through a mixing console recreates a larger space and makes our brains perceive the sound as much bigger, and less awkward, than it really is.

There are numerous ways to recreate reverb, from an actual reverb chamber, to spring or plate reverbs. But these days we primarily use DIGITAL REVERB. Digital reverbs seek to recreate an acoustic space through a mathematical analysis called an ALGORITHM. Basically, they analyze the behavior of soundwaves in different environments (like a large stone church, a concert hall, or a small carpeted room) and create a map of these sound wave environments (they call this an IMPULSE RESPONSE or an "IR"). Using these IR's and algorithms we can run any sound source we'd like into any virtual space we'd like. So if I want to hear what the snare drum would sound like if played in a cathedral, I can simply run the snare signal to an FX processor set to a "Cathedral" reverb setting.

## USING REVERB LIVE

**It's extremely IMPORTANT to note that when you decide to use reverb live, you are committing to pay full attention to turning it down if the singer begins talking!** It's very distracting if a sound person forgets to turn the reverb down when a singer is speaking or praying at any time in the set, so you must always be on your toes, ready to kill the verb instantly if need be.

## UNLOCK

**How much reverb should I use?** I always say that the key to using reverb live is to be SUBTLE. Remember, with reverb you are trying to add a natural ambiance and space to the sound, so it should sound natural unless you intentionally want it to sound like they are singing in an empty water tower. An easy way to do this is to turn the reverb up until you can hear it, then turn it down a notch. This makes sure that it's there, but tucked away to seem more natural.

## DELAY

Delay is another often used effect as it also helps us create depth in our mixes. Delay gives us the feeling of space, but with the key element of time. Delay is the recurrence of a signal over time, like an echo in a canyon where you say "Hello!" and wait for the sound wave to reflect off the surface and return to your ears with a clear "Hello!" The original delay effects were created using reel-to-reel tape recorders, then they transitioned to analog circuits, but today, as with reverb, we primarily use digital synthesis to recreate any delays we like.

## USING DELAY LIVE

Like reverb, be sure to mute the delay when someone is speaking, unless you are intentionally trying to add some serious dramatic effect! Also, most FX processors today have a TAP TEMPO feature, and you should use it! The tap tempo allows you to sync the repeats of your delay with the tempo of the song. You do this by tapping the "tap tempo" button to the beat of the song for two or more beats (depending on the model of processor). If the band is not playing to a click track then the tempo will fluctuate slightly throughout the course of the song, so you'll need to re-tap the tempo during the song to make sure the delays are still in sync. Just as with reverb, don't overuse delay, if delay is on too many channels, your mix will be confusing and headache-inducing. I like to use it on the lead vocal in songs where there is space for the delays to be heard.

## OTHER FX ON THE PALETTE

### OVERDRIVE AND DISTORTION EFFECTS

Overdrive is the sound created by additional overtones being added to a signal through the clipping of a signal. These effects can range from light overdrive to heavy fuzz.

The story goes that the first guitar distortion was created by accident, (and so goes most of the stories pertaining to FX creation: a random accident, someone mistakenly plugging a device in backwards, etc. I guess no one ever intentionally sets out to invent a new effect), but it is by far the most commonly used guitar effect.

It seems as though our ears, in accordance with our sinful nature, find the addition of complex overtones more interesting to listen to than a pure and simple sound wave.

79

### MODULATION EFFECTS
Uses a slightly delayed signal to add motion to the sound. Common examples include: Chorus, Phaser, Flanger, Tremolo.

### FILTER EFFECTS
Primarily uses fluctuations in EQ to create an effect. A Wah-Wah is a primary example.

### PITCH BASED EFFECTS
The sound created by altering the pitch of a sound. Vibrato, Octave, Harmonizers, and Auto-tune are examples.

### UNLOCK
Tremolo or Vibrato? Sometimes these two words are wrongly used interchangeably, but the confusion can be easily clarified. **Tremolo uses changes in Volume** (amplitude) to create the feeling of movement while **Vibrato uses changes in Pitch.**

## *Conclusion*

For decades renowned electric guitar players have crafted their signature sound with the use of effects. Since their hands are busy playing guitar, guitarists generally use the types of FX processors you can activate with your foot (and therefore called "stompboxes"). Whether they have a single stombox or a plethora, guitarists have discovered the value in taking a sound and creating something interesting and original through the palette of FX. In like manner, you as a sound sculptor should be creating and shaping your sonic art through the use of your FX palette. Remember, effects are not only in your tool box to create far out sonic experiments, they can also practically assist you by simply making your mix sound more full, balanced, and natural. If you haven't delved into the world of FX processing then I highly recommend you start today.

# NOTES

# *Section 10.*

## GETTING EVERYONE
## ON THE
## SAME PAGE

If the key is to be distraction free, then we must discuss the single most distraction-prone piece of technology in our services: Lyric Presentation.

## BEGINNING

I remember it like it was only yesterday, having a large box of file folders containing the alphabetized collection of overhead transparencies that was our worship song database. Some songs were hand written on the transparencies using a dry-erase marker, others nicely printed from the ink-jet printer at the church office. The person running transparencies had to be on their toes, keeping the right lyrics at the top of the screen at all times, sometimes a song had two-pages so you had to be quick in the transition, all the while keeping an eye out for pesky moths and other flying creatures drawn to the bright light of the transparency machine. I am SO glad those days are behind us! When the church gathers we come to worship corporately, meeting together to worship our Savior with one voice, as one body. Foundational to that purpose is that we all be on the same page, singing the same words. Today we have the convenience of connecting a computer to a projector or flat panel TV and not having to worry about moths! Unfortunately, the modern conveniences haven't eliminated all distractions, in fact it might be worse than ever. Distraction-free lyric projection takes preparation, attention to detail, and focused service.

**First you need to have a proper functioning lyric projection system which would include:**

**A Computer with additional output for multiple monitor mode:** You must have a setup that allows the operator's screen to be independent of the church's main screen. This will give the operator the ability to make changes and adjustments without being a distraction.

**Software:** Don't tell me you are still using PowerPoint for worship slides, please don't tell me that! If so, you must make it priority #1 to get software that is actually designed for worship lyric presentation, believe me, IT IS WORTH IT!! If you need to do a media ministry bake sale for a month do it, raise the funds to get legit software, you'll be glad you did within a couple of services. I highly recommend ProPresenter software by a company called Renewed Vision. Within a week of transitioning from PowerPoint to ProPresenter I felt like it had already paid for itself in the amount of time, stress, and distraction it had saved.

**Projector or Large Flat Screen TV:** Whatever suits your meeting room. Make sure people in the back can clearly see the screen and that it is bright enough even in the middle of the day.

**Proper Cabling:** The current video standards for cables are HDMI and DVI, with HDMI being more widespread and also having the ability to carry audio.

**A human operator with a heart to serve and create an atmosphere for worship.** Whenever I train someone in running the lyric software I let them know that they will be leading the congregation in worship just as much as the worship leader on stage. I look for people who have a heart to serve the congregation through facilitating corporate worship. It really helps if they are also detail oriented, able to focus, and a worshipper who is familiar with the songs the band is playing.

---

Once those pieces are in place, we come to the actual slides themselves. It only takes one typo on a slide to send people's minds rabbit-trailing off of Jesus and on to who-knows-what. So I've come up with four questions to ask when it comes to the layout, format, and look of your lyric projection slides.

---

**Four Very Important Questions to Ask Yourself:**

### #1) Is It Readable?
Can you clearly read the text, even from the back row of seats? If not, then what do you expect those people to do during the songs? Crochet?

Are words spelled correctly? Typos on slides are inexcusable. Some people don't let it bother them, but other people are like the scribes of Jesus' day and can get really distracted by the smallest jot or tittle.

Are you spelling the right words? This is a biggie. In the day and age of spell-check and auto-correct we hardly bother to see not if the words are spelled correctly, but are we using the right words? The best example of this is with "there" "their" and "they're", three words that sound the same, are spelled right, but CANNOT be used interchangeably because each word has a completely different meaning. The same goes for "your" and "you're", "presence" and "presents", or its and it's. Spell-check will not tell you if you are using the right words so it is critical that all slides are inspected before every service to make sure they are correct.

I see these mistakes all too often, and there are times where it's not just a typo, the re-defining of a phrase due to the misuse of a word can sometimes lead to heresy on the screen! One time I saw a slide that was supposed to read "I love Your presence" but instead read "I love Your presents", suddenly the song went from being about the beauty of intimate times with God to being about Christmas gifts!

### #2) Is it Consistent?
From one slide to the next and one song to the next the slides should be consistent in terms of capitalization, punctuation, colors, fonts, and backgrounds.

**Capitalization:** Are you going to capitalize the first letter of each line on a slide? Will you capitalize the "You" or "Him" if it is speaking of God? Whatever your church decides, you must be consistent with it on every slide, or else people will be confused and distracted.

**Punctuation:** Will you use periods, commas, colons, semi-colons, exclamation points, etc? You probably shouldn't try to use periods and proper grammar in song slides because the songwriting medium is not one for perfect and complete sentences. I recommend you not worry about punctuation at the end of each line or phrase on a song slide. It also helps the slides look less cluttered. But whatever You do, be consistent with it.

**Colors:** Choose a color that can be easily read, especially against the color of your background, so people don't have to strain to read it. Also, don't change font colors on every song. A key point to remember with media presentation is: **JUST BECAUSE YOU CAN DO SOMETHING DOESN'T MEAN YOU SHOULD DO SOMETHING.** I've seen some horrific font colors that were almost unreadable, just because you can change the font color doesn't mean you have to.

**Font:** make sure it's readable and not drawing attention to the font. The purpose of worship lyric presentation is not to show off how many great fonts you have on your computer, if you have a wonderful font that is very readable then great, use it and be consistent with it.

**Backgrounds:** Yes, I know you just received a free download of the "1,000 Must-Have Church Slides Collection" and you are excited to use them all, but please remember, the purpose of the media is to focus people on Jesus, not focus them on the media. So when you change between backgrounds every 45-seconds it starts to get a little overbearing, even in the attention-deficit age in which we live

#### #3) Is It Worshipful?

As I just mentioned, with the focus of worship being our Savior Jesus and not media creation, it is healthy to ask: are there any fonts, backgrounds, or motion graphics that are distracting people from focusing on Jesus? Sometimes playing the video file of an eagle flying through a canyon while we sing "You lift us up on wings like eagles" is a little over the top. We don't need a visual representation of everything and having too much motion going on can take our minds off of the One who is worthy of all focus! So unless the media is intended to be the focus (and there are those times), it's best to just keep it simple.

### #4) Does It Flow?

As I stated earlier, changing the slides is really leading worship, the timing by which you change the slides is almost like conducting a choir. You want to make sure the slides are changing at the proper time: neither too soon (or the people won't know the last words of the previous slide,) nor too slowly (or else they won't know the words coming up in the next slide). Also, it helps if the person operating the software is familiar with the songs so that they can know how the song with flow in terms of structure and arrangement. There will be occasions where the person can't find the right slide or maybe even the right song altogether, in this circumstance it is better to simply leave a blank screen up there than to try and force a half-correct slide or flip through a bunch of wrong slides. Better to just go to a blank background and let people listen to the words than watch a barrage of slides fly across the screen.

## *Conclusion*

Lyric presentation is an essential ministry to the church body, putting the church on the same page in worship and allowing us to raise one collective shout of praise! But, like sound, it is a ministry that needs focused people who will commit to putting in some time beforehand to plan, prepare, and proofread.

# NOTES

## Conclusion

Well, there you have it. What you have just read is a conglomeration of information I have learned through the years by means of classes, co-workers, books, countless articles, and countless hours of practical experience. I know I am still a student in the technical arts and will be as long as I'm breathing. Even so, I hope you have been instructed and encouraged through the pages of this book. Now that you have a stronger understanding of the foundations of audio, can speak the lingo, and aren't afraid to get your hands on the equipment, I hope you will dive in headfirst to gather the most important piece of the puzzle: EXPERIENCE. Keep doing it, keep learning, keep training your ears to identify frequencies, keep stretching yourself and your mixes and you will see continued improvement for the glory of God.

You now also have another responsibility: to teach others what you know. The technical ministry is not a Lone-Ranger ministry. If you try to do it all yourself, you will get burned out. So, train up others! Jesus is our prime example in this and even if you don't feel qualified to teach someone else about audio, you must do it. Simply show them what you do, explain to them why you do it, and then go from there. I've added a basic checklist in the appendix of practical tasks that you can use as guideposts for training others. You will be amazed at how much you learn from teaching others, and you'll see that the ministry works so much better when we function as a team, remembering that the church is a body made of many different organs.

## Conclusion

As stated in the introduction, I believe that the people serving behind the scenes in the local church are instrumental in its world-changing mission. The most vital organs of the body are those unseen, and the same is true of the body of Christ. So use what you know to be used by the Lord. There is no task too small, for the need is so great. Because faith comes by hearing, and hearing by the Word of God, then our desire should be to let the masses hear the Gospel of Jesus Christ that comes from the Word of God. Ultimately, our time in this life is short, so I will repeat Paul's prayer for you as you wisely invest your time in working for the Kingdom of God!

"Therefore, my beloved brethren, be steadfast, immovable, always abounding in the work of the Lord, knowing that your labor is not in vain in the Lord."

1 Corinthians 15:58

*Thank you.*

To my wife Emily and daughter Chloe for your daily love, laughs, and support. You are the most beautiful and tangible blessings in my life.

Dave Shirley for planting the idea in my head to write a book.

Scott Cunningham and Robin Lewis for your encouragement to finish the book.

Josie Tennison for your patience and perseverance throughout the project, your hard work and creativity are a blessing beyond words.

Diane Nash for lending your amazing proofreading skills to the project.

Kate Adams for giving your time and input to the project.

To my first audio instructors Darren Bowls and Scott Vance, your mentorship has been invaluable to me.

Rick Greene for giving me my first opportunity to teach a sound class.

Jeremey Wilson and Eddie Cruz for being my sidekicks in ministry the past eight years.

To all of my CCBC Sound and Recording students over the years, it's been a joy and honor to serve as your teacher!

To all of the wonderful staff at Calvary Chapel Bible College whom I've had the pleasure to serve alongside, it is truly a blessing co-laboring with you all.

**Lord Jesus for providing me the opportunity to walk in the abundant life only You give and for the all-sufficient grace that displays Your strength in my weakness.**

===

## Bibliography & Recommended Resources:

**The following resources have been helpful in my growth and/or have also been useful in the making of this book.**

Davis, Ron. *Live Audio Basics* DVD. Central Point, OR: Down 2 Earth Audio, 2005
    A great DVD set for training volunteers. Whereas many audio training videos are dry and tedious, this set makes it interesting and watchable, while still getting the content across.

*"How Loud Is Too Loud"* Dangerous Decibels.org; www.dangerousdeci-bels.org/education/information-center/decibel-exposure-time-guidelines/
    Charts detailing SPL levels and exposure time limits.

Rat, Dave. *Microphone Rejection Nodes*; www.ratsound.com/2009_12_02_po-lars.htm
    A helpful online article in regards to microphone polar patterns.

White, Glenn D. *The Audio Dictionary*. Seattle: University of Washington Press, 1991.
    This is a great resource for finding concise yet thorough answers to your audio terminology questions. It is no longer in print, but worth picking up if you can find it.

White, Paul. *Live Sound for the Performing Musician*. London: SMT Press, 2003.
    A thorough examination of live sound principles and an all-around great resource for your library.

# THE SOUND GUIDE TRAINING CHECKLIST

## STAGE SET-UP

- [ ] Understand and use a Stage Plot & Input List
- [ ] Set up a mic stand without stripping it
- [ ] Run cables with slack at mic stand and/or monitor
- [ ] Correctly set up and aim monitors
- [ ] Make sure the stage is set neatly (cable & stand organization)
- [ ] Properly mic all drums in a drum kit (Kick, Snare, Toms, OH's)
- [ ] Properly mic a cajon/percussion
- [ ] Properly mic an electric guitar amp

## SOUND CHECK

- [ ] Line Check all inputs and channels
- [ ] Know how to use the talkback mic
- [ ] Set gain on all channels (unmute, fader up, gain up)
- [ ] Eliminate Feedback (using gain, mic placement, & EQ)
- [ ] Test and dial in a podium mic, lapel mic and/or headset mic
- [ ] Demonstrate proper communication with stage musicians
- [ ] Demonstrate a proper attitude & level head in a stressful situation

## CREATING A MIX (BALANCE, EQ, FX)

- [ ] Add compression to kick drum, a vocal, & a subgroup
- [ ] EQ the kick drum, an acoustic guitar, & a vocal
- [ ] Add reverb to a vocal, snare drum and/or cajon
- [ ] Create a balanced mix with vocals on top
- [ ] Check the SPL's of your mix using a dB meter

## STRIKING THE STAGE

- [ ] Properly disconnect an XLR
- [ ] Properly disconnect a Speak-On
- [ ] Break down a mic stand with out stripping it
- [ ] Wrap Cables using the Over/Under method
- [ ] Unscrew a mic clip in the professional fashion
- [ ] Demonstrate proper understanding of where/how equipment is to be stored and secured.
- [ ] Demonstrate the proper order of powering up and powering down the system